MALACHI O'DOHERTY

# I WAS A TEENAGE CATHOLIC

*Malachi O'Doherty*

*15 · 11 · 03*

In memory of my sister Brid
who died on her fifty-first birthday
28 April 2001

*Red and yellow black or white,*
*Jesus doesn't give a shite,*
*Jesus loves the little children of the world.*

# Prologue

I was lost. Street lights and reflections in wet tarmac were in one confusion. I was back at a roundabout I had circled twice already before I saw the sign.

Harryville was an unlikely name for a part of an Irish town, more like a nickname, but there it was. I took the main road passing through, with no plan but to look out for other journalists who would know me from events we had covered. The dangerous part would be walking to the church from wherever I could park my car, and walking back to it later. There would be police cover at the actual confrontation; there always was.

There was a town car park on my right. Was I too exposed if I parked in the obvious place? Before I got out, I rigged up my microphone and mini disc recorder, setting it to record with the pause button on. There would be no fumbling. I knew people would be aggressive and it was their aggression that I wanted to record. It would be pointless to introduce myself and get chased, or worse, kicked, and have no broadcastable sound at the end of it.

Further along the road, I saw the array of forces. The other journalists were in the church grounds, with their cameras and recorders, safe behind the police lines. About two hundred policemen and women stood with their backs to the church, facing the mob across the street – about thirty men, women and children gathered on the footpath, shouting abuse and trying to be heard inside the church itself.

The soft lighting behind the stained glass windows suggested a demure service inside.

I had seen before how dangerous occasions like this evolved into manageable patterns. Here the police would be content, so long as the road was kept clear for traffic and the church itself was safe. The mob would know the rules governing them, rules imposed by their own controllers, not to throw anything lethal or give the police occasion to attack them, by for instance blocking the traffic. The logic was simple; it wasn't just about keeping the standoff calm, it was about reserving definable steps of escalation and withdrawal.

I went first to introduce myself to the police.

'I'm a journalist. I take it I'm free to move about as I please here.'

'Of course, Malachi. Just don't block the road.'

I was getting used to people knowing me. I appeared occasionally on television and I had a photo by-line in the *Belfast Telegraph*.

I crossed to the crowd then, before I had time to lose my nerve. They soon surrounded me.

'Hello, I am a journalist from the BBC. I'm working with the *Sunday Sequence* programme.' Much of my journalism was in Religious Affairs, and in Northern Ireland this included some of the most violent and contentious stories. I had been drawn to religion by accident, but it suited me, not just my interest in following sectarian conflict, but also a curiosity about those who were believers. This extended even to the fanatics, for I had known religious fanaticism as something normal and close all my life.

I had grown up in the fundamentalist Catholicism of the 1950s and I had lived for four years – before taking this work – in an ashram in India, drawn I suppose by the same curiosity that had me here. Now religion was less an experiment on myself and more a field of work in the world. I wasn't looking for God, and if I was following those who did, it was not in order to be more like them – as it had been with my Indian guru, Swamiji – it was just to get good quotes from them for reports that I made for *Sunday Sequence*. I didn't define my interest in religion, but just let it lead me. I rationalised it as simply an area of journalism that was as interesting for me as sport or theatre might be for someone else, but then journalists who specialise in sport or theatre tend to engage for personal reasons beyond the ability to earn money and merely enjoy themselves. I liked religious journalism because the God question – in whatever form – seemed to go to the heart of what people found important.

Your God says a lot about you. In India I had found that Hindus have a huge range of god images to draw on, and that it is perfectly acceptable to devote yourself to the elephant-headed god Ganesh or a goddess riding on a swan (Saraswati), and that none of these are in competition with each other. They are picked for their gifts, in the way Catholics pick saints to offer special devotion to. Northern Ireland Protestants exercise similar choices, between gods which are judgemental and strict, or merciful and tolerant.

Often my reports had no religious people in them at all. An early one covered an Orange ceilidh that Loyalist paramilitaries helped organise in Moneymore. The Loyalists felt they were losing the argument with Irish Republicans, who had a language and a culture and said that it was in defence of this that the IRA shot policemen and bombed shops and bars. Paramilitaries with a culture could more easily make the argument that they were fighting for the self-determination of their oppressed people. The Loyalists wanted to be able to put up that kind of argument too. They were taking on culture, the way I was taking on religion, without feeling much at home in it, but with a sense it would ennoble them anyway.

I was remembering how that story developed when I approached the Loyalist mob at Harryville. I had learned from it that some of the nastiest sectarianism can incorporate a sense of fun. That night, in Moneymore, I had been called to draw a raffle ticket. The prize was a clock made by a Loyalist prisoner. The winning ticket had been bought by my producer, Terry Sharkie. It went down badly.

'The taigs have got the clock! Fenian fix!'

The crowd were stamping their feet and yelling at us. Leaders of an organisation which routinely killed Catholics to express political protest gathered round us, assuring us we were welcome to stay. A woman even asked me to dance.

This humourless Harryville crowd only wanted rid of me.

'What the fuck do you want?'

Perhaps I was putting too much faith in the sense of humour I had observed before in violent people.

'Who'd he say he is?'

Swamiji was my model of restrained response. Faced with a direct threat, I would still try to express something like honest curiosity.

'He's a fucking fenian.'

He was also my model of someone who kept his mind on his objectives. I wasn't there to defend my dignity but to record Loyalist aggression on tape without actually getting kicked or head butted. This was working so far. I didn't need sensible answers.

'What is the purpose of this demonstration?'

'You're lookin' for a kickin', I'm telling you.'

I could select no single interviewee. I would have felt safer if I had identified the man in charge and gained his attention. On the night of the Orange ceilidh I had kept as close as possible to

Andy Tyrie, the moustachioed boss of the Ulster Defence Association, reasoning that befriending one killer might not save me from others, but that befriending the man in charge would save me from all of them. That night Tyrie knew that I was nervous, and toyed with me. Some of the heavies close to him – men who had killed Catholics – made crass banter, like little boys bragging in front of their father, but it was a night off from violence.

I trusted that similarly here in Harryville, someone was in charge and had defined the limits. The men kept jostling and more would push from behind to get close to me and start again with the same question.

'Who the fuck is he?'

'Show us your press card.'

I wasn't going to risk losing a press card, but I had business cards I could give them. These didn't have my home address on them, just phone numbers and an e-mail address. I gave them one of the cards. It told them the most important thing they felt they needed to know.

'He's a fuckin' fenian.'

'You're one of them, you cunt.'

'What is the purpose of your demonstration?' I asked.

'Fuck off.'

I looked down then and saw that the cable from my microphone was no longer plugged into the mini disc recorder. One of them had pulled it out. I should have had the sense to wear headphones, and then I would have known when I was recording and when not.

We had spilled out onto the road now, and this was what the police were here to prevent. There was a loud bang, like a shot. The protestors were cheering before I understood what had happened. One of them had dropped a firework near my feet. He could as easily have stuffed it down my shirt or trousers.

'Fuck off. Is there something you don't understand?'

So I crossed the road, away from them, and they did not follow me. They were like trained dogs who knew the boundaries within which they were free to move.

The senior police officer was clearly amused, but asked me not to draw them onto the road again. I went into the church grounds to meet Alan and John and Moira and half a dozen other journalists and camera people that I knew. They were soon round me to ask if I was all right.

'You're a braver man than me,' said Alan, who fed stuff to CNN. Then I listened to the disc and realised that I had very little of their abuse recorded. I would have to go back into the mob.

I could hear the mass inside the church and worked out that it was about half over. The mob across the road was shouting swear words, and occasionally a name, presumably the name of someone in the congregation. When they saw me, they shouted louder, and I realised it was better to stay out of their line of vision, if only for the sake of the congregation.

It was a cold evening. A large drunk man arrived to speak to the protesters. He stood in the middle of the road and some of the others came out and gathered round him. Alan said he thought this was a senior Loyalist, a key player. The police appeared to have calculated that it would be less fuss for them if they did not try to move him. I checked my equipment was ready, checked my heart for fear, and went over to try and interview him. The crowd started shouting, 'fenian bastard' at me, but the man seemed to be trying to listen and to understand me, and when the others saw this they dropped their voices out of respect for him.

'Why have you chosen to picket this church?'

I knew the answer already. It was a counter-protest to pickets on Loyal order parades in Dunloy, fifteen miles away.

'Uh?'

'Why have you decided to picket this church?'

A little boy of about ten was hanging close, enjoying the glory of standing beside one of the big Loyalists. 'Fuck,' said the boy. Then he shrieked the words that would make mine the best report of the night's events: 'It's not a church, it's a fenian hole.'

With that, I didn't need to record more voices, so I let the drunk Loyalist mutter some nonsense into the microphone, thanked him and concentrated after that on recording background noise and colour. I went up to the porch of the church when the congregation was singing the communion hymn. It was a good spot. I was safe. The shelter of the porch kept the wind off my microphone. There was a nice echo there. And the mob was still yelling. By moving deeper into the porch, and out a little again, I was able to find the point of balance at which I could record both the music and the shouting. I stood there, with my headphones on and listened, first as the careful expert, thinking about sound quality and editing problems. For instance, I wanted a good clean passage of music with plenty of abuse, but with no audible fucks. I did not want to have to bleep over any of this, and I did not want to have to make cuts in the noise of the rabble that would break the rhythm of the singing, recorded on the same track.

Then I was listening, not as a professional monitor, but with emotion. I am wary of religious feeling in myself, having overindulged it in youth and in later religious phases I've gone through, like my spell in India with Swamiji. I wonder if it only comes over me when I am vulnerable. I have a sense of the tone of indulgence, the pitying whine that betrays mock piety, and I refuse to seek out wonder or reverence, only accepting them when they overtake me, despite myself.

I had made myself emotionally impregnable to face the mob, and now that I was safe in the porch, I relaxed into a sensitivity that surprised me, as a child might, weeping in bed after a hard day, not quite knowing why.

'Sweet heart of Jesus, make us know and love thee … '

Make us know and love thee? As if the condition of knowing and loving God could be foisted upon me, as abruptly as a shove from a thug. It was decades since I would have thought myself a Catholic. Was I religious at all? I was sometimes. I had been as devout in India as I had been as an eager little boy. I still had the imprint of that on me. My heart knew the responses of a devout person, even if I had no theology.

'Sweet heart of Jesus, font of love and mercy, Today we come … '

That is what the congregation was singing, and the mob was shouting louder when the church door opened.

' … O touch our hearts, so cold and so unfaithful … '

The survival of the music was important. Never sure that I believe in God in a way that I could communicate to another person of faith – if we got down to comparing credos these people would probably take me for an atheist – I still believe in faith, that it is a decent and beautiful thing.

'Fenian bastards! Fuck the Pope.' Some of the congregation were coming out and the mob recognised individuals.

'Declan O'Loan. Fuck Declan O'Loan. Fuck Malachi O'Doherty. Fuck the Pope. Fuckin' bastards. Fuck yis.'

They were shouting randomly, not chanting, so most of the actual words were indistinct. I was able to mask the fucks in my recording by moving deeper into the porch and closer to that beautiful absorbing music.

'Sweet Heart of Jesus, make us know and love thee ... '

On an ordinary day I would not have sought comfort in that church with that music, and its power to move me in my adulthood would have embarrassed me. Here it was the answer to barbarism.

PART ONE

I grew up in an absurd religious context. I was conditioned in a faith which really does not exist anymore, except in the bones of my generation. This was pre-Second Vatican Council Irish Catholicism. A devout guilt still clings to me as a hangover from that childhood and the strange religious education that was imposed by teachers who seemed not to be as devout as they wanted us to be, and who were too callous to consider that at fifty we still might bear emotional scar tissue from their contradictions. A child who is taught to love and to surrender and is then confused by adult temper, starts out on a long quest to resolve innocence and candour with a wariness of violence and cynicism.

The education my teachers gave me in mathematics hangs on to bother me in the same way. When I add figures, say for my tax returns, I still mouth the little instructions of my primary school teachers. When a column has gone over the ten and the ten has to be added to the next column left, I whisper the words that Miss McRandall taught me: 'Carry my one'. I cannot add without doing this and I still cannot make a moral decision without having to explain my reasoning to the Father in Heaven. I am burdened with the presumption that I am judged.

The Father in Heaven, as I have assimilated the idea of him, is nothing like my real father. He has nothing to do but wait till the end of time for my answers. 'Why did you kill the little shrews? Why did you not stay with Linda and marry her? Why did you run away from Belfast when the shooting started, when I might have had plans for you? What was so wrong with having a steady job? Were you too good for that sort of thing too?' The Father in Heaven has the list of my failings. He knows what to accuse me of. My own father? He knew too.

My earliest memory has a biblical resonance, full of astonishment and fear. In the back garden of our house in Ballycastle, close to a ditch of briers, Little Me is watching my father trying to lug a sheep out of the tangle. I am small, and this is big. My father's footing is insecure, and he can hardly grapple with the frantic beast.

13

The sheep doesn't know that the clutching man is trying to help. It is stupidly wrestling deeper into the ditch and the danger. Daddy, or Barney as the men called him, is cut and bleeding. There are white scrapes like ash on the skin of his arms and legs, and stripes of bloody perforation. He is fighting his own rage and frustration, slipping into the ditch and losing hold of the sheep; probably containing curses because children are there. The curses, had he been free to roar them out, would have been: 'Jesus Christ al-fucking-mighty. Fuck, you bastard! Fuck!'

I retain just a picture. There is no memory I can trace on either immediate side of this incident. Probably I hobbled over to the commotion and was drawn back from the edge of the ditch. In this picture, what worries a little boy is that he has discovered limitation. His father is strong, but not strong enough for a sheep. He has seen the paradox that animal panic and desperation only make things worse. There is the other paradox of generosity in my father's violence. This memory resonates with the story of Abraham and Isaac, as if I worried even then that I might have been in the thicket in place of the ram.

The words I put on that experience now are words I didn't have then, of course. I had only a sensation, a tremor, only a bodily acquaintance with awe, reverence, fear. I had never seen masculine strength fully drawn to the point of failure before. A thunderstorm could hardly have been more worrying.

Left to dwell on these things alone, I might have imagined a god like Zeus, who had temper and limitations. I have the trace of a memory of something as awesome, the first sight of the sea; probably coming to it through the town of Ballycastle and over the hill. What could I have made of it? All I recall now are the later sightings, when at least I knew what I was looking at, the giant glinting heave of blue, that is more like the sky than the earth. I imagine my mother said something like: 'It's the sea. Isn't it beautiful?' Yet every time I look at it now, from a car, say, when it comes into view from a distance, I feel a remnant of the forgotten shock of my first seeing it, when telling me what it was, told me nothing.

In those days I was a pagan. Well, not strictly. I had been baptised, twice, once in urgency lest I die, being frail and premature and one of twins, when you expected one twin to die. My brother was saved, according to family lore, by St Anne's water. We were baptised a second time more formally, when older than usual. The story is that I spat out the salt that the priest put on my tongue. This was a natural response from one who could have had no faith other than that smeared on the brow and on the lips by a priest's hand. My way was cleared beyond Limbo, straight into Heaven, a Heaven I had no thoughts about, or interest in, yet.

When we were small, we lived in Ballycastle, and my father went to Belfast to work in a pub on the Grosvenor Road. He came home every Wednesday, for work was busiest at the weekend. What was life like then? I remember only that we were glad to see him. A child loves daddy, even when afraid of him. He is a man of ferocious moods, who expresses even affection through scowls; who can turn on you, particularly if he is annoyed with your failure to read his mock gruffness as playfully intended. Early in my life I began a special relationship with powerful men. I have an ambivalent style in relation to them. I start with ingratiation and end in betrayal.

Strangely, however, God was not just Father but Child too, they said. Religion was as difficult as subtraction. I could not follow what the nuns in school were talking about. The anomaly would be explained as 'a mystery'. Indeed the mystery was greater still because there was a third, The Holy Ghost, who wasn't like the ghost who frightened you, 'ghost' being just a word for spirit, and who works quietly to inspire you, and particularly to inspire the Pope.

The age of innocence in which we were free to be fuddled by details, gave way to one in which details were so important that ignorance of them might be thought a state of sinfulness.

'If the Pope was handing out sweets at the church, you'd all be down there like a shot, but there is someone more important there, giving away something better. The Lord Jesus himself is giving grace to those who worship him, and yet you walk past the church as if its sanctity means nothing more to you than the smell from a butcher's shop.'

That was what the teachers said. The boy who took them at their word went to the church and prayed, nearly every day, for years. If their message was credible, that there was something better than sweets to be had there, I would still be going. I expect I would find my old teacher there too if he himself believed what he expended so much wind and passion on.

I was a religious child. I was a sanctimonious child too. A lot of children, particularly girls, seemed to have worked out that religion can help you to win a quarrel, or at least to complicate one.

'That's mine!'

'No, it's mine.'

'No, it's not, it's God's. God owns everything.'

The only way out of that argument is to say you don't care whether God owns it or not. That would be too dreadful a declaration for a small Catholic child of my generation.

I'm told I had a very early habit of breaking crucifixes. I had said I was pulling Christ off the cross so that he wouldn't die for me, but I wonder if I was really challenging God at that early age. There were a lot of broken crucifixes about the house, for years, usually on old rosary beads that could not have been decently put in the bin. I was held to blame for them all.

As a child, the important thing was to master the sign of the cross, and to learn off the questions and answers in the catechism. 'In the name of the Father': Miss McRandall's hand takes a wide sweep, full length out to the side, and up to the brow. 'Amen', the hands are now pressed flat together with the thumbs crossed, in front of the sternum. Yet, though we were impressed with the importance of the posture, we could see that others had settled for a more casual presentation. We had a little Lourdes grotto at home which showed even Bernadette's hands joined slackly, the fingers curving.

'It's different for her. She's allowed to do it that way,' said my sister Brid. 'You're not.'

Adults in church seemed to bless themselves in a hurry, just bowing the head and quickly marking out the shape of the cross in front of them, as if they were pointing out the parts of the body to themselves, checking that they were still there: there's my head, there's my chest, there's my shoulder, and there's my other shoulder. People commonly made the sign of the cross every time they passed a church, some furtively with their thumb on the brow, as if they might just be wiping something off. You had to bow your head when you mentioned the name of Jesus. That holy name was the most important word you would ever speak, and you must never speak it in vain.

Once in class, we were going through the catechism and came to the question 'Why do we call God just?' A nervous boy with a speech impediment replied: 'We toll Dod dust … ' and the whole class burst out laughing. We were mocking him for his difficulty, but more, we were horrified that God had been inadvertently insulted. Our whole training was to be on guard against the inadvertent sin. This one risked bringing the wrath of Heaven into the room, and when the wrath did not come, life seemed suddenly a little more free and easy.

That old catechism is still being printed and sold, even though it has been superseded by the Second Vatican Council. I read in it: 'Must everyone belong to the Catholic Church? Everyone must belong to the Catholic Church and no one can be saved, who through his own fault, remains outside it.' That little catechism also says: 'We should pray with a humble and contrite heart, with attention and perseverance, with confidence in God's goodness and resignation to his will, and in the name of Jesus Christ.'

My first confession and communion are so far back in my memory that I can hardly find them. We lived in Belfast by then, and I was five years old. The first confession was an early example of the difference between warning and result, and taught me that laws do not have to be observed too strictly. Have you lied or said a bad word? Then you might go to Hell. You are as bad as a murderer in the eyes of God, for you have offended him. It is the teacher who looks a fool when this is refuted by the priest; when you go into the side cubicle of a confession box, to share soft whispers with him through a grill, and he gives you a prayer to say and tells you that you are a lovely boy.

The teacher had told us that we must always make a good confession, and clear up all our sins. Then we would be pure and holy and fit for communion. After the first communion we would be radiant souls who would go straight to Heaven if we died. This is a dangerous thing to tell a little boy if you don't want him to be smug. I told the priest, as I told one every two weeks for the next ten or twelve years, that I had told lies and harboured bad thoughts. I thought a bad thought was something like coveting a brother's toy or planning revenge. Sinful humour then was about shite and God. Jokes were about bare bums, or saying 'Oh Jesus'; bawdiness was taking the Lord's name in vain.

I would hear my father often say: 'Oh, Jesus, Mary and Joseph, give my head peace'. Or an exasperated teacher would say:

'God, give me strength'. So there was disagreement among adults, it seemed to me, about which usage of the holy name was sinful, and which not. I actually almost never told lies; I would have had a happier childhood if I had done, and my bad thoughts seemed not my own. Sometimes I stumbled into sin on a pun or spoonerism, and said something rude: 'Rise and shite, breakfast's ready', I would laugh with thrilling mischief, but I always tried to correct my manners, like a good boy, and not linger too long in a state of gracelessness with the eye of God on me.

'That's a sin for you saying that.'

'Mammy, he said a bad word.'

Jung says he discovered neurosis when he found himself as a boy unable to follow the inclination of his humour which imagined God's throne in the sky as a commode. God was having a shit, a wholly untenable thought for a child disciplined in a religious culture. I asked my mother at bath time if angels had bottoms. Did you have to go to the toilet when you were in Heaven? You could get into difficulty trying to limit yourself to good wholesome thoughts, and those moments, when your sense of humour and imagination sneaked through the boundaries, were shocking but liberating. And your poor mother had to find some way of explaining that angels can eat all they want but never have to shite. 'It just disappears inside them. It turns into holy air that smells like roses and seeps out through their skin.'

'They don't even fart?'

'No, and you shouldn't either.'

'Have you indulged these bad thoughts, my child?' I had no idea what the priest's question meant. I suppose he wanted to know if I was in constant war against the invasion of prurience into my pure young mind, or whether I passed on such smut as occurred to me.

Bawdiness was a boy's liberation. 'My daddy can smoke through his arse. I've seen the nicotine stains on his underpants.'

You laugh and you survive. The lightning does not strike, and in time you realise that there is no spiritual penalty for free thinking. I would spend a year in my twenties reading nothing but pornographic comics to find that same sense of liberation, to tear away at the restraints against thinking or saying anything I could imagine. My moral education would be to pull away at the barriers erected against humour and freedom of thought, yet I am still surprised occasionally by how the mythologies of childhood stick to me.

One stormy day huddled in our living-room, I asked my father what caused the thunder. I was bewildered and fascinated by his answer: 'It is the clouds bumping together.' But surely, daddy, the clouds are just steam.

'Ah, but when they are that big – it is a big noise to us, but a small one to them.'

He had the gift of telling a story like that with unreserved seriousness. Years later, in a storm, I was walking home with my nervous older sister, Anne. There was thunder overhead. 'What is it,' she said, 'that causes the thunder? I mean, I know it's the clouds bumping together, but what else?'

She had not till then questioned what our father had told her when she was seven years old, as he never questioned even into old age what his own parents had told him, that the peat bogs over Ireland were the residue from the Flood.

Perhaps we all live by these unquestioned mythologies, some of which would disintegrate if exposed to the air. I discovered one in myself. When Roger and I were very small, we were given new berets to wear to school and disliked them. One of us had the idea that we might post them home. We stuck them in a letterbox. Indeed, they did come home – which was not what we had secretly wanted – because in a small town, postmen can work miracles like that. I had a nightmare about my beret. I dreamed it was on the top of the spire of the old church and that I had to climb up for it. This, I suppose, dramatised my fear that I would have to seek it out myself next time it was lost. Probably my mother had said something like: 'Be thankful I don't send you down to the post office to get it yourself' – or worse – 'I've a mind to post you in the damn letterbox if you don't appreciate the money that is spent on clothes for you'.

I have always assumed without question – because this was never in the forefront of my thinking – that Roger and I both had that church spire dream, that the dream itself was a shared experience. It was only in recalling the incident for retelling that that anomaly occurred to me, otherwise it sat comfortably in my mind as one of the fundamental assumptions that make me who I am, the twin that I am.

On the day after my first confession I made my first holy communion. Roger and I were dressed in little white cardigans because my mother could not afford new suits for us. White was for the state of grace we were in. The eucharist wafer stuck to the roof of my mouth but I was not allowed to peel the soggy flake off with my finger. In those days, only a priest was allowed to touch the wafer with his hand. We believed the sacramentally transubstantiated bread had sacred properties. We had heard stories of evil men taking it out of their mouths and wearing it close to their bodies as a shield against danger when they robbed banks. The abused wafer had bled with sorrow. I left it in my mouth to dissolve. It was like a sherbet sweet called a Flying Saucer, but dry and stale to the end.

We joined the communion parade up the Andersonstown Road and we were the most conspicuous children there, with our matching distinctive woollens.

'Ah, look at the wee twins', we heard the people say from the side of the road. That became a taunt from Brid to annoy me, even years later, 'Ah, look at the wee twins'.

She meant: 'You think you're holy do you? You're a frigging hypocrite.' She denigrated any pretension to moral superiority in me; just the antidote for a smug wee boy, such as I had been trained by my teachers to be.

The school encouraged us to give up sweets for Lent, to set up a little altar to the Virgin Mary during the month of May and to ask our mothers and fathers to say the family rosary at night, if they didn't already. A mother of six children would struggle to resist that demand. The school raised a collection in class every day for the Black Babies Fund, and during Lent for the White Babies. You had either to ask your mother for money for the funds, or give up what little sweet money you had. The school waged occasional campaigns to get us to go to mass every morning, or at least on every first Friday of the month. To attend mass and holy communion on nine consecutive first Fridays was to be assured of a happy death. I once asked a teacher if that meant that you would go to Heaven, even if you had just committed a mortal sin, and he said: 'Well it wouldn't be a very happy death if you didn't.'

Death was the focus of this religious culture. We were being taught to live our lives aware of death and the danger of Hell. Why bother about God? Because you die. This is a strong incentive to stay with the faith; lose it and you have to find some other way of coping with mortality.

My granny died when I was nine years old, and the headmaster at assembly asked all those boys who had missed the first Friday mass to put up their hands. I, of course, being a smug fool, put my hand up. I probably expected sympathy for the excuse: 'Please sir, my granny died.'

'Your granny died and you didn't go to mass,' he yelled at me in front of 700 other children.

'What sort of child doesn't go to mass when his granny dies?'

That taught me to be a little more wary both of fishing for sympathy and volunteering information that could get me into trouble. That's how my moral education progressed, but I was a slow learner.

Sometimes I didn't speak up when I should have done. When Father Cunningham, the parish priest, went into hospital and was expected to die, the teacher encouraged us all to write letters to him. He had recently given us a sermon at Sunday afternoon devotions about St Joseph the Worker. This must have been late spring. Joseph was an example of manly humility. He was the one who got least credit. I composed my own prayer to St Joseph to endorse this virtue of humble labouring, and sent it with the letter.

When he came out of hospital, recovered and not yet a saint after all, Father Cunningham stood on the steps of the school before all the boys and girls assembled in front of him, in separate groups, of course, and thanked us for our letters and prayers.

He said he was particularly taken by a prayer to St Joseph composed by one of the boys. He didn't say who had composed the prayer. Perhaps he hadn't remembered my name or been able to read my signature. Before we were even back in our classrooms, word had gone round the school that somebody else, one of the cleaner, brighter boys, had composed this wonderful prayer which had been acknowledged from on high for artistry and purity. I was too embarrassed to argue the point then, which must say something. Perhaps, even then, I had a sense that a boy writing prayers for the parish priest was ingratiating himself more than was really decent. I learned that day to keep backup copies.

Our school, The Holy Child, was governed by ideas of infantile saintliness. The girls' half was overlooked by the sweet St Maria Goretti, who had been raped and stabbed; not that the coarse word 'rape' actually featured in accounts of her ordeal. There was little communication between the two sides, though one day my sister Brid's teacher took her out on tour round other classes, including my own, to sing a song that she had impressed her with.

Brid was lithe, blonde and beautiful then. Her favourite song was 'Two Little Orphans'. 'You must hear this,' said the teacher at the door, escorting Brid in, and our own master told us all to be quiet and listen, while Brid, treated to more attention than she had ever had in her life before, poised herself to plead from the heart:

> Two little orphans, a boy and a girl,
> Sat by an old church door,
> The little girl's tears were as fresh as the snow
> that fell on the dress that she wore.

Brid was sentimental all her life.

The boys' half was dedicated to poor Dominic Savio, who had mortified his young flesh for Christ's sake; who should be an example to us all, who slept with walnut shells under his sheets. I fostered fantasies of my own martyrdom, perhaps because that was all I could ever imagine my teachers would approve in me. I would stand against sin and my little friends would beat me to pulp and I would go to Heaven. Gunmen would hound me into the church and I would take the chalice from the tabernacle and throw my body over it, and their bullets would cut into my back with a warm, sensuous glow.

One afternoon, playing in fields near where we lived, I saw a group of boys and girls intently occupied in some game in a circle they had made of cut grass. They chased me away when I looked closer. I caught a glimpse of somebody's bare bum. One of the girls who had been most dismissive of me had taken down her knickers. She scowled at me, 'fuck off'. Some vague sense I had of the sexual economy, presumed that it was men who told women what to do, not the other way round. My strongest thought, however was theological. These children did not believe that God was watching them. I couldn't have shown my bare bum to anyone, knowing that He was watching me. Fear of God didn't restrain them at all. Therefore, they did not believe. I had never before even considered an option of not believing or thought out what glorious opportunities might come with contented atheism. I had wondered at the bravado of the young people who used bad words like fuck and shite in God's hearing, and thought they were simply reckless.

I prayed every day in life when I was a child, and enjoyed praying. A Catholic child of my generation was taught a basic repertoire. There were the two special morning prayers; the Morning Offering and the prayer to the Guardian Angel. 'Oh my God I offer thee all my thoughts, words and actions ... '

The point of teaching us this, as was explained by teachers and priests, was to regulate behaviour. If you offered everything to God, then you had to show commitment and follow the proper form. 'Oh Angel of God, my Guardian dear, to whom God's love commits me here, ever this day be at my side, to light to guard, to rule and guide.' Religious observance was a form of self-policing. I wanted to ask if the Guardian Angel was there all the time, even when you went to the toilet, but that was not a question you could ask.

Often, after school, my brothers and I went into the church and prayed at the altar rails. My prayers were conversational rather than formal. I talked to God or the Virgin Mary. I reported to them my feelings about my life, my anxieties and my quarrels; but I also felt a more universal responsibility and prayed for the conversion of Russia and China and for the soul of Oliver Cromwell. I prayed in bed at night, curled up under the blankets in preference to kneeling on the cold floor.

I prayed with passion sometimes. My father brought home a little puppy once and locked him in the coal shed, where he howled for his freedom, and this tore at my heart such that I could barely distinguish between the dog's emotions and my own. I went to my bedroom and said a rosary and pleaded with God for the dog to be happy.

There were three gigantic Catholics in my childhood. These were: two popes, Pius XII and John XXIII, and President Kennedy. I was only nine years old when Pius died, and yet I followed the progress of his illness as if he was my own grandfather. I was awe-struck to hear that he had spoken directly to Jesus while on his death bed. Could it really be true? As pope, Pius was the emissary of God on earth, so if anyone actually got direct answers from Heaven, it was surely him. I understood that the Pope was infallible in pronouncements on faith and morals, and I realised that logically he must have been receiving direct instructions.

While I had a compelling child's fascination with the story of Pius' relationship with God, I also had a powerful sense of attachment to him as a spiritual leader. In everything I did for days, whether playing in the fields or trying to get to sleep at night, my thinking was overshadowed by the horror that this man, whom we loved, was about to die. Yet, how could his death be bad news if he was going to Heaven?

'Could a pope go to Hell?'

'Surely,' said my mother, 'if he was a sinner.'

'But if he was a sinner, he wouldn't really be pope, would he, because he wouldn't be delivering God's messages to Catholics?'

My mother was what you might call spiritually pragmatic. She wanted me to believe in the Catholic faith. She also wanted me to have a bit of normal human savvy and not be taken in by pious frauds, of whom there were plenty. Conspicuously devout people were to be regarded as suspect, whereas those who didn't go to church were not to be judged bad people on that account alone.

'Mummy, could I be pope some day?'

'Well, you would have to be a priest first,' said Brid.

'No you wouldn't,' said my mother. 'If God wanted you to be pope, he would call you, whatever you were doing.'

'But you have to be an Italian to be pope,' said Brid.

'If God calls his pope, he can call anyone.'

Anyone!

Hour by hour on the day he died, I waited for news of Pius, and in the afternoon the wireless said he had passed peacefully away. He who had been with us was now with God. What would they be saying to each other? Pius would be reporting on his work, but God would know already what he had done. They would not have anything to say to each other! Nothing! This seemed a shocking thought.

I wondered too about John, when the white smoke rose and declared that he had been selected by the cardinals to replace Pius.

I wondered how the Holy Spirit had guided their choice. If the Holy Spirit chose the one he wanted for pope, why did the selection take so long? Why did he not just write the name on the wall with a ghostly hand? Why not settle a tongue of fire over his head? How could this be an election and yet an appointment by God? But the proof of the choice was that John was such a holy man.

I worshipped him too as an awesome spiritual figure. I even wrote him a letter and asked him to pray for Irish freedom. I was ten years old.

The most magical day of the Catholic year was All Souls' Day. That was the day you could release someone from Purgatory into Heaven with an Our Father, a Hail Mary and a Glory Be. We would go to the church and there would be a jotter page with a penned list of the names of the dead of the parish sitting on a black-draped coffin. We always wondered if there was an actual corpse in the coffin. The rule was that each soul required a separate visit and recitation of the prayers, so we would walk into the church, examine the list, say the prayers, leave, then turn at the porch and go back in again. After a few visits going down the list, we realised one year that we were all praying for the same people.

'They should have some way of ticking them off, so that you don't waste time praying for some that are already done,' said Roger. It was always embarrassing when he thought of something I hadn't. It made me feel that I didn't measure up to him, and if you don't measure up to your twin, you feel you don't measure up to yourself.

'Prayers aren't ever wasted,' I said, more unctuously, but I could see the logic. What if the people at the bottom of the list got left out, because no one did enough visits to get down that far? We picked five each, and then went home feeling that that was enough people released from the fires of Purgatory for one year.

Prayer was also like keeping a diary, or like addressing a fantasy friend to whom anything could be said. The only adult-approved private space was the quietness around you when you prayed. Later, when older, you could bring shame into that dark corner, or go there to express gratitude, when there was no one specific to thank.

To stay in a state of grace a child had to make good confessions regularly but one day you had to choose between confessing a sin that is too shameful, or living the tainted life of the unshriven forever. When that moment came to me, I didn't realise that

I was making a choice for life, that I was learning to be secretive and encrusting my soul. For me, the first sin that was too horrible to relate was the killing of small animals.

I had been playing in fields near our home on a summer day. We rolled an old oil drum to the top of a hill and chased it down again. The grass was long and scorched yellow. The field had been left untended, probably to become a building site the following year. As we stood breathless round the old oil drum I heard a faint squeaking sound.

'Shush! Listen.'

I put my ear to the itchy grass and heard the birdlike cheeping of small frightened animals. It seemed to come from somewhere deep and impenetrable. Our shuffling about on our knees did not break the shelter over them. This was far more interesting than an old oil drum. This would be a story to tell. Little boys boasted, in those days, about their grasp of nature, not about their knowledge of cars or football teams. I rummaged and tore into the grass to see what was there.

'We shouldn't be doing this.'

I had to claw deep and tear more and more tangled grass away, surprised the hole was so large and well covered and realising that by the time I was deep enough to see what was there, it would be impossible to repair the damage and leave the spoiled nest.

'The mother will not come back now,' said Roger.

So, I decided, we would have to rescue the little creatures we had disturbed. They were five little blind shrews. They were the colour of dried blood, and naked, and you could see the veins bulging under their skin. They wriggled and squealed together in a frantic bundle. I lifted one and nursed its quivering little body, held the wee face to my ear and listened. What would we do? I indulged the fantasy that I was like a nature programme presenter on television, who had a right to handle small vulnerable things like these. Then I shared out the little shrews and the blame for taking them among my friends and we each took one home to nurse and feed, hoping our mothers would share in the wonder. My mother was furious.

'You can't feed that. It won't eat anything you give it. It is supposed to be with its mother. It was all right where it was. Have you no sense?' I put the frightened and docile animal into a cardboard box in the back yard and left a little saucer of milk and some crumbs and a pile of grass for shelter. I would nurture the shrew. In the morning it was dead and dry. All the others died too.

'That,' said Mum, 'is the worst sin you have ever committed.' It was therefore the first sin that I held back. I never made a proper confession again because I never could say plainly that I had brought death to those little things and confusion to their mother, who I imagined was still fretting round the hole in the field.

'You will tell that in confession on Saturday,' said my mother. I couldn't. I never did.

If Heaven or Hell awaited me after my death, depending on the state of my soul, there was, I sensed, another world dangerously close to me already. It was not Heaven or Hell but still, a region where ghosts moved. It was intimated by that feeling on the stairs at night that someone is right behind you; the horror of being alone in a large house; the fear with which the contemplation of the other world can drench you.

There is a story remembered in our family of a time when I was about five years old and refused to go upstairs to bed alone in the dark and my mother asked me what I was afraid of. 'Lions and tigers,' I said. I surely didn't believe that there were big jungle cats waiting for me behind the bathroom door. No, they were waiting for me inside my mind, and in the dark my imagination would be the only reality for me.

There was a way of scaring yourself too. Posing as a ghost or an evil thing, contorting your face, tightening your cheeks, enlarging your eyes, curling your lip. I have a scary face that I tease children with now, and yet I can still feel sometimes a sense of being possessed by a glad idiot spirit when I enter that grimace, as if I might stay there and my sanity might never come back.

At Hallowe'en we heard stories of the banshee and the fairies, but I was not intrigued by them. The devil was real enough, but he seems only to have been a petty power, that could have been outwitted by a child's prayer and good intentions. The old famous ghost stories were commonly told among children, of the hitch-hiker who disappeared in the car, the card player with the cloven hoof. I think I always had a sense that these were the mere soap operas of the other world and not convincing intimations of terror. The real thing was the notion that crept up inside you, that overtook your mood, the chill, the unutterable sense that there was a stranger standing very close.

At fifty, I still occasionally find myself on the stairs, returning to bed from the bathroom at three in the morning, in the dark, affecting detachment from a fear that I know will block my path if I admit it.

Along with puberty came an amplification of that sense of dark danger close at hand. I often saw vivid pictures behind my eyes before I fell asleep. This astonished me the first time it happened. The detail suggested something seen in a real way rather than something imagined. I would never be able to consciously create images like these, though I tried in meditation in India years later. If I try to recall a picture or a photograph that I know well, I never get the whole thing as I did with these, which were as plain as if they were there, not normal memories at all. Sometimes they were horrible. I would be looking at the face of a person, not knowing who, and the attention that I would give in staring at it would contort the expression into a grotesquerie, as the eyes enlarged and the grin spread. The image seemed an automatic device, outside of me, using my own attention against me, reflecting it back to me distorted.

One of the things that we were encouraged to avow we would never do was deny our religion. The scenario was this: you would be held at gunpoint and asked to deny God, and you would refuse and die a martyr. Bobby Hanvey has written hilariously about this, in his book, *The Mental*, so this must have been a recurring obsession in Catholic education. There were two dangers: Communists and Protestants. Either might challenge your faith. If they did, there was only one respectable course open, and that was to die with God's name on your lips, as so many had done before you. Just knowing that you would do that, if you had to, made you a better person.

The fantasy that you might have to follow St Peter and a string of others into martyrdom became more tangible against the background of Northern Irish sectarianism. I learned early that you might indeed be challenged to say that you were a Catholic and face a penalty. The first occasion for me was a confrontation with a little boy of my own age, about eight. He prodded a knife at me with: 'You're a fenian, aren't you? You're a fucking fenian.' I knew what a fenian was, historically, which is probably more than he did, and I was able to say in all honesty that I was not one, nor had I ever been one, nor did I believe, indeed, that the movement was still extant. My just being an unctuous smart-aleck little Catholic annoyed him further.

Did God really expect me to let that little boy stab me? Well, that's what we were taught in school. I was developing a conscience that relied on more than what I was taught at school. In little ways like that, I found that the teaching of religion clashed with instinct and simple good sense, and had to make way before them.

There has always been a strange dissonance between what Catholics say they believe and what they really believe. My favourite hymn as a child was 'Faith of Our Fathers', a tribute to Christian martyrs, which contains the lines: 'How sweet would be our children's fate, if they, like them could die for Thee'. Did people of that generation really think that it would be like an answer to a prayer for them if their children were raped and slashed with knives, or turned on the spit or burned at the stake for their faith? The hymn they sang in church declared it was precisely that which they wished for. They stopped singing that song a decade later when their children were being killed for being Catholic, as hundreds were.

We can look back at the Catholic popular literature of that time and be embarrassed. The final chapter of *An Outline History of the Catholic Church* by Reginald F. Walker provides an example of Catholic fundamentalist arrogance in the generation which preceded mine, which produced the men and women who taught me as a child. The book received the Catholic *Imprimatur*.

Father Walker's God is a God of vengeance who has punished the world for lack of faith. That's what the Second World War was for.

'God,' he explained to Irish children, 'is but permitting men to suffer the direct logical consequences of their revolt against Him, to reap the terrible harvest of their own sinful sowing, and to drink the bitter chalice of their own misdeeds.'

Father Walker had an explanation for the suffering. 'If men must tunnel in the earth to find themselves a shelter, it is because they have rejected their true religious home in God's plan for their lives.'

Protestantism was to blame for that war: 'The crash of ancient and majestic cities into bloodied ruins is but the outward result of the gradual inner collapse of all religious beliefs and moral standards of right and wrong in the non-Catholic world since the Protestant Revolt.'

Roman Catholicism, in Walker's vision, 'takes the shock of assault unmoved'.

He is confident that 'though all else should fall, [there is] one great fabric against which cannon will thunder in vain and which will stand when the Maginot and Siegfried lines have crumbled into dust – the Catholic Church.'

Father Walker was not an eccentric conveying a silly notion. Thomas Merton, one of the most respected liberal Catholic theologians of his day, wrote very similarly. In *The Seven Storey Mountain*, he blamed the Second World War on Catholic parents who did not send their children to Catholic schools. After professing himself 'overwhelmed at the thought of the tremendous weight of moral responsibility that Catholic parents accumulate upon their shoulders by not sending their children to Catholic schools', he says, 'Catholics, thousands of Catholics everywhere, have the consummate audacity to weep and complain because God does not hear their prayers for peace, when they have neglected not only His will, but the ordinary dictates of natural reason and prudence, and let their children grow up according to the standards of a civilisation of hyenas.'

The school's fear of Protestant opinion overshadowed one of the most joyous occasions of those days: the opening of the local library. Our teachers had built up our apprehensions about the library with stern lectures about how we must behave in this new place. They were challenged by the arrival of the library themselves, for it was not going to be under their control. Their fear of it seeped through everything else they did, and added to the general air of wonderment. We were bewildered that something would be built so close to the school, and for the use of the children, and yet that the teachers themselves would be uneasy about it.

On the day the library opened, dozens of us swarmed round the door to get in. The building was like a little bungalow in its own grassy grounds, off Slievegallion Drive. It presented an almost physically intriguing allure. I stood at the back of the crowd, perhaps only inadvertently lending weight to the impression of an unmanageable rabble. None of us individually thought we were doing anything wrong. The librarians were so worried they locked up. They must have waited inside till the crowd cleared. I went home without a book.

Father Cunningham was furious. He called a special mass and ordered that we be processed to St Agnes' church to hear the sternest rebuke. 'Shame on you,' he roared from the pulpit. 'Shame on you.' But for what? There was a sin here that I did not recognise. He laid down the order that we would, in future, be escorted in groups to the library by our teachers, and would otherwise stay away. We would queue at the door. We would be filed in, and when we picked our books, we would take them to the teacher, who would approve them as suitable or send us back to the shelves with them. This arrangement did not work out just as neatly as he intended, however.

Inside the clean new building, which smelled of polish and fresh print, I saw that there was an adult section, where danger lay, and a children's section, which was much smaller, and which I suspected wasn't entirely suitable for young minds either. The woman at the desk was relaxed among all this spiritual danger. Nor did she seem frightened of us or horribly offended. Thinking about her now brings to mind a chirpy woman in a chemist's shop in Belleek who once sold me a packet of condoms. 'Threes or twelves, dear? Sure you're as well with the twelve.'

Her appearing at ease with the radical idea that children might want to ransack shelves of books for joy, made her suggestive to me of a larger world than the school had ever implied. My first book out of the library was about the pyramids of Egypt. Mr McEvoy checked the cover, flicked the pages and permitted me to take it to the counter. Other boys gathered up their books and showed them to him. All their rebelliousness had gone. They would acknowledge the authority of the teacher and the parish, even inside the walls of this free space. That is all that was required of them.

Mr McEvoy must have felt like a fool there. He was not an assiduous censor. He was too self-conscious to notice when my brother Roger bypassed him with a book of his own choosing. Or was it that he was simply unable to exercise authority there and knew it? Roger had discovered that when there are two separate governing authorities at work, like Church and State, you are free to simply take your pick between them.

The book Roger took was about Africa, and had pictures of naked tribes-people inside. That's all I remember about it. That and the horrified whisper of the boys of our class outside: 'Roger O'Doherty has taken a Protestant book out of the library.'

Teachers saw it as their role to police the loved and forgiven children of God. They acted in contempt of the very principles they taught, as if to let us know that forgiveness and God's love were for later. Old Testament rules applied in the classroom. I had a teacher in primary school who beat me across my palms to improve my handwriting. He might as well have punched my ears to improve my hearing. Yet I had no choice but to think well of these people and their efforts for me.

Once on the day one little boy started school, I was showing off to him how well I was liked by the teacher, playing football with him after class. There was about a dozen of us running around on the black tarmac on a grey autumn day, chasing the ball and enjoying a sense of being favoured by 'Sir'. Suddenly someone was shrieking. I looked round and saw the same teacher beating the new boy about the head. This five-year-old had approached the teacher to ingratiate himself too, and called him a fat fish. I watched the teacher batting the little boy's head with the flat of his palm, as if trying to wipe something off it with the most cursory contact, backing away from him, repelled. The chasm that was opening for me was the prospect that I was to be the enemy of the teacher, if I sided in sympathy with the screaming child, but the only tenable option before moody power is to adapt to the power and presume always that the victim is in the wrong.

An older boy like me, protective of the younger one, in that situation says: 'Are you stupid? Why didn't you keep your mouth shut? Have you no sense. Go and apologise.'

It takes an adult to blame an adult.

There was a culture of abuse then, a culture of contempt for children. There was a wide vocabulary for the different types of hitting. 'I'll box your ears. I'll smack you. You'll get a clout. I'll cuff you.' These were the terms of teachers and parents. Boys confronted one another with threats in different language: 'You'll get a dig in the bake/a boot in the hole/a toe in the bollocks/your pan knocked in.'

My friend Anne is visiting us with her little girl of five, the same age as the boy who was walloped about the head. The girl has the same eagerness to play. 'Malachi,' she says, to distract me from her mother, 'you are a rotten egg.' What would happen if I was to respond to that by slapping her head, like a ping pong player rehearsing his stroke on her, until she was squealing with shock. Would Anne say: 'You have a way with children, Malachi. You should be a teacher'?

As children, we recognised easily that punishment was the product of mood rather than righteousness, and learned to negotiate it. We would rage quietly against the injustice of it, but it would never have occurred to us to call it abuse or that one day it would be banned.

At the age of eleven, I went to secondary school with the Christian Brothers, who were famous for their discipline and their dangerous rages.

Young men no longer see any attraction in joining religious orders. Why train to be a teacher and work full-time in the job, sharing a home with the same people you work with, all of them men, surrendering a salary to the order itself? For most people, that is an image of Hell. At least a priest is revered by a community. His domestic world is ordered round him in his own house by attendants and, if he believes in his ordination, he feels sanctified by Holy Orders and permitted to mediate between God and his parishioners, to relieve them of their sins and bring them into communion. The brother has none of these benefits. He is simply a teacher who can't have sex and has to share his home with the people he works with, who are all men who can't have sex with anyone either.

Yet they are still held in some regard. I have written and talked publicly about the violence of the Brothers, and been rebuked for my disloyalty in doing that. Chief among the things they say to me is: 'You have to allow for the fact that things were different then.'

Do I?

I will not now go back in my mind to the classroom where Brother Gibbons strode among us with his cane and his miserable grated cawing, and feel the respect for him that I felt then. I can allow that they were perhaps trapped by circumstance, but they were not all fine decent men behaving according to the mores of the time; they were men cornered into crowded classrooms with dozens of boys, and they became children themselves, often nasty children.

I have repeated this same strange conversation with people who think I should not criticise those teachers.

'That's the way it was in those days. You should be grateful for the education they gave you.'

'Why? It was the law of the land that I had to be educated. If they hadn't been there others might have done a better job.'

'Other schools were as bad.'

'Perhaps they were.'

'You exaggerate. We all had to put up with it. It didn't do me any harm.'

'Well, each to his own memories of it.'

'And yours weren't the worst anyway. I remember one Brother who used to punch boys in the face for fun. I remember one who used to make boys take their trousers down for a beating.'

Those who say you shouldn't talk about the past invariably end up telling stories of even worse abuse than I remember.

I don't remember everything. I remember things like summer and sandals, those brown leather buckled shoes with their white spongy soles. I can smell them by memory and I can feel the light relief of walking in them after a winter of heavy, tight-fitting brogues. A child's sensuous pleasures can be revived in memory after forty years, but much else cannot, if it wasn't really understood at the time. C. S. Lewis, describing the school he called Belsen, tells of Oldie, a vicious master, and yet concludes that boys are never as oppressed by those over them as by their peers. We never really wanted to understand the teachers or sensed we could. They were always remote.

There was an incident after one of the lay teachers had beaten me. He heard that I had called him a slob, when talking about him on a bus, and he wanted an explanation. He took me aside and waving a little flat stick, as if he might hit me with it, asked me to explain why I had called him that. I didn't consider that he was seeking some assurance from me that I respected him. I was a boy. I had nothing to say to him but what my boy's mind might imagine he would want to hear. It didn't impress him. What he wanted, I think now, was to cross the barrier between friendly teacher and wounded wary child.

I was trained by my slappings to be afraid of teachers, to ingratiate myself with them where possible and to take advantage of them furtively. He was wasting his time.

Brother Gibbons looked like the image of St Gerard Majella on a little medal I wore round my neck. He was a skinny man with a coarse voice. His facial skin was pallid and blotched, and he had the nickname Scabies. His head was almost like a bare skull, bulbous above, pinched below. Someone gave him the name Kipperhead, and it stuck. If you look at dried smoked kippers, opened up on a plate, you can see the eye-holes.

Brother Quinlan was Primo, after the big-eared mouse that advertised tea. There was a degree of affection in that name. Mr Watson, a lay teacher, started out as Winker, after a character in *The Dandy*, and quickly became Wanker Watson, after his probationary period had expired without him persuading anyone to like him. I almost never used those names. I had not the courage to hate Brother Gibbons. I feared him, and I feared that he might detest and reject me. Therefore I loved him.

'You're the size of tuppence and you've the cheek of ninepence, O'Doherty,' said Gibbons. When boys had to go to the Brothers' residence, they often asked me to knock on the door and do the talking, for I had the neck for those things. I welcomed opportunities to show off before powerful men and at the same time to contend with them. The closer you get to a scary man and survive, the less power he has over you.

Brother Gibbons came into the class on the first day we had him, to teach us Latin, and he charmed us with his humour. He teased us and seemed a frail and malleable man who would be the least of our problems in this daunting new school. Education seemed easy when he recited a few Latin words, all ending with a, for us to remember, Regina, Agricola, Mensa, Casa. He constructed a quiet world in which queens and farmers and tables interacted with each other, and in which nothing else really existed.

Next day he came in and gave every boy in the class one slap on the hand with the leather strap for each of the words that had slipped his mind overnight and that strange world's importance was violently impressed on us. From then on we would have to believe in it and know it intimately. We now knew that Kipperhead was the biggest problem we had in life.

I crouched in my desk, rubbing my burning hands together between my little thighs and the boy next to me whispered: 'Don't let him see he's hurt you, Doc.' I wasn't sure that sort of defiance wouldn't bring even greater wrath down on me. When I got more confident, I would contest the punishment. One of my teachers once hit me with a cane. The frayed end had been wound up in sellotape. He missed my palm and scraped a bleeding welt on my wrist.

'Sir, sir, you cut me!'

'Sit down, O'Doherty.'

'Sir, you're supposed to hit the hand. I'll tell Brother O'Connell. I'll get a note from my Mammy.'

'Sit down, O'Doherty, or I'll do it again.'

Other boys caught the scent of his vulnerability. He had wavered enough to reveal it. He wasn't confident.

'Sir! O'Doherty's bleeding.'

He had to make a show of looking at the scraped skin and saying grudgingly that he hadn't meant to cut me, that the wound would heal quickly, that I wouldn't bleed to death.

Teachers expressed different things about themselves through their handling of their weaponry. Brother Quinlan carried his strap folded in a loop in a voluminous pocket accessed through a side slit in his soutane. He drew the strap out slowly, as if handling something that was a danger to himself too. He would set it on his case on the table and leave it there as he walked among us. I would watch it unfold like a live thing, wondering if it would ever fully straighten out on its own. He was a decent man and rarely beat anyone. When he did strike, he struck always in anger. He beat you as if he was furious that you had cornered him into having to beat you.

Like Wyatt Earp, the Dodge City Marshall, with a Buntline Special, Kipperhead needed an instrument tailored to his own technique, a custom-made, experimentally verified instrument of pain infliction. Dowelling rods, he found, had less spring in them than the canes and hurt more. They didn't fray at the ends. The strap, designed as a more humane weapon, would leave red welts but would not disable the hand. The swipes at the tips of our fingers stung horribly on cold mornings. The more blunt thwack of a stiff rod hurt the bones. He liked to acquaint us with his readiness for violence at the start of a class by asking a boy to go to his office or another room and 'fetch for me my stick'. Kipperhead often thrashed boys in anger, indeed in rages, but he thrashed us sometimes with humour and pleasure too. His caning was a dance, which was meant to impress, both with grace and accuracy. 'Hold still, boy.'

Boys had their different devices for managing a beating. A good caning requires co-operation from the victim. A boy with a cold hand will try to arch back his thumb, knowing the side of the knuckle there will sting more than the flat of the hand. Some would drop the hand as the cane or strap landed and move with its sweep to lighten the impact. Some would twitch their arms in anticipation of the slash and hardly find the resources in themselves to hold still and take the pain calmly. In some this was nerves, in others an effort to time the retraction of the hand to coincide with the swipe, hoping that a teacher who kept missing would give up. Since teachers genuinely believed we were stupid; they might give up on demanding that a boy hold his hand out properly. Others boys felt they best defeated the anger of a teacher by holding the hand out firmly, defying the blow. A boy might let his arm hang limply at an angle to his body, so that the swipe of the cane or strap would glance it rather than engage it at a perpendicular. One teacher might counter this by grasping the wrist and holding the hand firm for the lash; another might accept the challenge to inflict what pain he could anyway at the awkward angle. Yet another might scowl, 'Hold your hand out boy or I'll give you a double dose.' One teacher might tap the hand underneath with the stick or strap, to order the boy to raise it higher, without a word. Another might punch a boy on the chest: 'Don't trifle with me, or it will be the worse for you'.

The Catholic tradition suspected children of a sinfulness they would not have understood. Perhaps there were boys in my class who felt appropriately addressed by all the rantings about smut and deceitfulness, but I think most of us did not.

The Brothers valued the basic education above anything higher. Were they suspicious of academic success? Perhaps the truth is more that so few of them would have been able to take us any further than secondary level anyway. The thing they seemed most contemptuous of in boys was any show of cleverness. That is because they were not all very clever themselves. They praised physical achievements more. A boy could be a great footballer without falling into the danger of getting above himself. Kipperhead would stand by the race track on Sports Day with a long stick to beat us across the legs to make us run faster. That was his way of making men of us.

This was a period in which men were allowed to oppress children, to demand both submissiveness and physical courage of them.

Some boys had the freedom of thought to despise Brother Gibbons and that appalled me. Imagine coming to the school with your mother, and her swiping an arrogant teacher across the face with her handbag. I have seen that. Imagine dwelling on your misery and scowling bitterness at them. What a fearful void that would open to childhood contemplation! I could not contemplate the void, therefore I had to accept Brother Gibbons and respect him. True powerlessness is the inability even to think ill of the one in charge. Yet in class I watched an unhappy man. I listened to his absolutist determinations of spiritual right and wrong, and I knew that they clashed with the more moderate voices.

'It will be worse for you if you leave the faith that you were born into, than if you were born just an ignorant heathen, for at least the heathen has the excuse that he never had the truth in the first place.'

No one else spoke like that but his was the more accurate reading of the catechism we had been taught since we were five years old. Brother Gibbons was fond of frightening generalisations. 'Think about this: two boys in this class will be dead before the rest of you are men. That's the law of averages.' Actually the number was higher, because of the political violence from the late 1960s.

We had him for the first two years in secondary school, for Latin. Then we had a blessed year without him and in fourth and fifth years he took us for maths and religion. In the year of grace we saw him only when he was patrolling the yard at lunchtime to make sure we were not fighting or smoking. Sometimes he even joined us for a game of handball. The only bat in this game is the palm of the hand itself. It is a form of squash, played with as many as half a dozen boys, before a broad brick wall. Gibbons was nimble and fast, even in that heavy soutane with the broad band at his waist and running down his side. He could sweep low to slap back an awkward ball. I have seen him fall and roll over on his back laughing. He was competitive and had little time for boys who were not playing to win. Play time was strictly punctuated however. When he clapped his large hands the fun stopped, and we lined up fearfully for class.

In my puberty, this was the man charged with teaching sexual morality, to a class of about 30 boys. We would read an imported American book that said prolonged kissing was allowed when you were engaged, but that necking and petting would only rouse the sexual urge and lead to sin. It seemed thrilling though that we were even talking about physical sex. No one asked him what necking and petting were, or what they were for, if not to lift the sexual urge. Our own vocabulary for physical intimacy had other words: lumbering and groping. I would have understood the book better if it had used these.

I often wondered what private spiritual life these men led. I never thought that they might be men like my father and his friends, the men of the street who tinkered with cars on a Sunday afternoon. I assumed that they were called by God to their life of service and that that made them superior. Beneath those dark dusty robes, did they sweat? Were they hairy? Were they clean? Superficially they were rough men. They had the signs of poverty about them. They carried old and battered cases into class, sometimes tied up with string. They wore old and flattened shoes, sometimes paper thin on one side of the foot. Their soutanes were brushed with chalk. Most of them had nicotine-stained fingers, which suggested to the imagination of a perverse boy that they had been poking at their arses. They mumbled their prayers.

Every forty minutes in school a bell rang to mark the end of a period, and the full class stood to say the Hail Mary. There were a few Brothers who seemed to do this without relish. Some just dropped their heads, and voiced the words into a large hollow chest. Brother Quinlan would face the statue of the Blessed Virgin at the front of the class and almost sweep us into prayer with the swing of his arm. Brother Gibbons demanded energy and concentration from our prayers. Prayer was punctuation of mood. At the beginning of the class a teacher would use it to settle us down and bring us to attention. The prayer at the end of a class signalled the freedom to relax.

What I took for holiness in these men was their remove, their uneasiness. They could be playful, if there was a ball at hand. There was little passion or levity in them; mostly just dry anger and dry humour. They had almost no informal social relations with people outside the order. Could they have wandered down the road, of an evening, for a pint in the Glenowen Inn? I don't think so.

I think they were even afraid to see us playing on the street, because they would not be able to whip out a strap and herd us into line. Therefore they would be at our mercy, though we didn't know it. I got a sign of that once when Brother O'Mahony and Brother Quinlan walked past us as we played with bangers. I threw one and the squirming, blue stick, spitting flame, rolled back into their path. They kept walking straight towards it. It exploded between their feet. They didn't break their step, and they never mentioned the incident afterwards in school.

The world which they described beyond Belfast was a dangerous one, a world in which we could lose our faith. In England, you could live years in the same street and not even know who your next door neighbour was, they said. The Communists were taking over too. There were more of them than there were Catholics in the world now. We had a responsibility to the poor, and to the missions. Years later I would meet the Christian Brothers in New Delhi, where they ran schools for the virtual Anglicisation of the Indian middle class and I wondered at all the big pennies I had given down the years to support that project. But parting with the pennies was an efficient way of acquiring a warm glow of self-satisfaction, so I cannot pretend I was the loser.

Kipperhead used his charm as manipulatively as he used his wrath. He could appeal to class pride and urge us to dig deeper into our pockets to raise money for the Missions. He could flatter a boy, but he could also tear him apart as viciously with his tongue as with his stick.

Walshy was the one you could sense had a genuine love of children. When we were only eleven years old he would sit in class and read stories to us from *Old Celtic Romances* by P. W. Joyce, 'Not by that other Joyce, that pagan. Not him.' I asked my mother to get me that book for Christmas. It was one of the first books I owned for pleasure. When I was sixteen I tested Walshy and drove him to the point of losing his temper, on the question of why priests were not allowed to marry. I brought him to a standstill and he conceded that we might agree to differ until faith and prayer would grant me more insight. How can you shed respect for a man who would concede an argument to a boy he has taught? I wish I had gone back as an adult and seen him before he died. I would have asked him why he tolerated Kipperhead's madness.

Yet I never hated Kipperhead as much at the time as I did later looking back, or another stupid teacher whose idea of a joke was to make a boy walk round the room shouting 'I am an Onion-head'. I believed in those people and believed in the religious structure they were a part of. I was a compliant child. I accepted that mood and misery played their part in the judgements of the Brothers.

Some boys in our class went off to Baldoyle in County Dublin at the age of fourteen to train to be Brothers themselves. What inspired them? Where was the attraction in a life of self-abnegation? Did they see themselves decades on, inflicting their own unhappy moods on another generation of boys in another city; pacing the aisles of the classroom, scowling at them: 'Amadan, fool, miserable child, have you not the wit you were born with?' I presume they saw themselves as closer to God, and freed from anxiety about money and relationships. The answer to all life's choices would be made simple: obey. Yet most of the later generations of Brothers left and now have children, jobs, mortgages and ordinary worries and they have that discomfited air of the onetime celibate about them, and that dash of self-importance that a man once called by God never seems to lose.

They had been inspired by Kipperhead, who had monumental rages against entire classes, who would line thirty boys around the class and make them hold out their hands while he thrashed them with his stick, howling as he moved among them, gyrating and sneering. Sometimes Kipperhead would torment a single boy by giving him 'a little warning', a light slap on the hand with the strap. This is the sort of thing he would do when he was in a good mood, even a little giddy. 'A little warning', beating him like that twenty or thirty times until the boy was on his knees weeping and Kipperhead was still smiling over his head at the rest of us to let us see that he was only playing.

What made his impressive madness explicable was the thought that he was working for us and that he was suffering in his holiness, and living by standards that were beyond our understanding, for the good of his soul. Maybe those boys wanted to be Brothers, thinking that then they would be able to understand him. We were relieved when Kipperhead went into hospital, yet the Brother who would replace him would have us pray for his recovery, and I would earnestly pray that the dear man would be well. I did not see his holiness as contrasting with his human rages; I saw them as part of the same thing. His suffering seemed a kind of holy martyrdom.

He was trapped. They all were. Imagine if Kipperhead had one day realised that his seniors in the Christian Brothers were not actually mediating the will of God to him at all; if he admitted that his own rages were born of his suppressed desire to go his own way. Imagine him putting on an ordinary shirt and jacket and walking down the Glen Road to an estate agent and asking for a flat or a house. Where would he have worked? What friends would he have had? The price of admitting that you are wrong is that you change your life completely, and that you own up to loneliness and a lack of purpose.

Kipperhead tightened his own chains for comfort and security, and insisted there was no escape from God's calling. Therefore the alternative life was not even worth thinking about. Later, there was a great exodus from the priesthood and the orders, when Catholic theology after the Second Vatican Council allowed people to answer to their individual consciences. This new spiritual freedom coincided in Britain and Ireland with an improved economy and an easing of traditional sexual restraints. A man in a dowdy habit who hated teaching could know that he might get a better job, keep his money and meet somebody nice. Even Kipperhead, in 1995, might have found himself working alongside an attractive woman preparing the May altars and felt free to invite her to have tea and a scone with him, and we all know where that might lead.

Two months, May and October, were given over to special devotion to the Virgin Mary. God himself was remote to us. Catholics tended not to reflect much on the Father. When Brother Walshe introduced the reading of the Old Testament that seemed a radical change. Jesus of course was God and was important. This was stated clearly in all discussions on religion, but really Jesus didn't occupy a central place, except in the reading of the Gospel at mass, which always began with the words, 'At that time … ' Mary was the one who counted, though the theology said that she wasn't God and was to be adored rather than worshipped.

Unlike a goddess, I suppose, Mary had been created by God and was born a human, but she was, we were told, born a human without taint of original sin, and she was also spoken of as having existed from the beginning of time. Nor did she decompose at death, but was lifted bodily into Heaven by the angels, which surely implies that her body was not the stuff of our bodies which would shiver or burn.

At twelve I joined the Legion of Mary. This was a prayer and good works group, effecting to be modelled on the Roman Legions. These groups were called praesidia. Primo, Brother Quinlan, was our spiritual director, but the president and the vice-president were men from the senior praesidium, appointed to look after us. There was a standard, like a totem, with Mary's image carved on it and the wings of the Holy Spirit above her, resembling the standard the Romans carried into battle. There was nothing militaristic about our Legion. We met and prayed together on Friday nights in school and reported on how we had performed our duties throughout the week. These duties might include visiting sick children or old age pensioners and saying a stiff little prayer with them. Or we might be put to collating the newspaper orders for sale in a cubicle outside the church after Sunday morning mass.

Our prayer in the Legion of Mary was the *Magnificat*: 'Who is she that cometh forth, as the morning rising, fair as the moon, bright as the sun, terrible as an army set in battle array?'

When I think over those words now I imagine a woman coming naked from her bed in the early light. They held a lustful fascination for me even then. Certainly the image was remote from the idea of the chaste and docile Mary of the demure statues, whose function was to elevate being used and obedient into noble virtues. 'Terrible as an army set in battle array'? This was a suggestion of a different, more interesting idea of womanhood and female power altogether. I could imagine some of the bouncy girls on the street as being 'terrible as an army set in battle array'.

One year the Legion of Mary organised a big ceremony at St Mary's church in Chapel Lane, Belfast and hundreds of us walked up in pairs, put our hands on the standard and took a pledge: 'I am all thine, my queen and my mother, and all that I have is thine.'

The objective of religious instruction was always to exact total commitment from you, so that you would surrender your own will to God's will. I was of an age to notice the dissonance between what people were expected to say they believed and what they really believed. I doubt if I even meant it then, but I wanted to be someone's, if not hers.

I led a coup inside the Legion of Mary. My first mischievous use of writing was as secretary of our praesidium. For weeks my friends and I dragged out a debate on a complaint made against us, that we had been messing around in the newspaper kiosk outside the church. I wrote extensive reports of all the points we made in defence and read them out week after week in the minutes, to be sure that I would have the last word on the subject. The praesidium, made up mostly of my friends, would accept the minutes and the chairman would have to sign them. If he aired any objection, I would challenge him and drag out the debate and then record that too for the next week's minutes, recycling the argument until others were sick of it. The only course I left open to them, if they wanted to end the argument, was to stop raising it and leave my version on the record.

Years later, on the London to Paris bus, I asked a black African about magic in his home country and he told me that he knew one group of people who were adept at spells and talking to spirits. 'They are called the Legion of Mary,' he said. I was never sure he wasn't teasing me.

The Legion reinforced the school's message that we should get our families to say the rosary every night. The family rosary, it taught, was what bound the Catholic community together. The motto of the rosary campaign was: 'the family that prays together stays together'. In our house we didn't ever succeed in establishing a routine of this for long. There would always be arguments about whether the television should be off or whether we could keep it on with the sound down.

You don't grow up with a very healthy attitude to women if you go to an all-male Catholic school where you are taught by celibate men and offered the Virgin Mary as a model of perfect womanhood, even if you are occasionally invited to regard her, in the words of the *Magnificat* as 'terrible'. The deficiencies of such an education leave you with basic learning to do later on. You leave school at the peak of your pubescent flowering and are permanently alert for sexual opportunity. All boys know the social difficulties that accompany the near permanent erection of the mid-teens. All boys have turned away to try to straighten the penis up behind the zip where it won't show. All I got from school to explain this was a biology book with a chapter on rabbit reproduction and a footnote to say that human sexual intercourse was roughly the same, though of course governed also by moral principles and a talk from the headmaster to tell me to wash my penis often but otherwise not to touch it. The teenage years provided little else than perpetual embarrassment.

For all their narrow moralising, the Brothers introduced us to girls, perhaps hoping to get us into sound Catholic heterosexual relationships early. They organised ceilidh dances for us through Irish language promotion. They encouraged us to speak Irish to each other at these, particularly at the Fáinne meetings every second Sunday of the month in the Ard Scoil in Divis Street. Perhaps they believed that if school-taught Irish was the language of our courtship, we would be well-mannered and formal in our dealings with girls and confined to using the words they had taught us. The night time ceilidhs, every few months in St Teresa's Hall, were much bigger affairs where we could meet the girls we had got to know through the Fáinne meetings and spend a whole evening with them, even walk them home.

There was no drink at these dances, and there was no conspicuous snogging. Yet the Brothers who looked in on us made clear by their manner that the rules were lax here. They approved of us pairing off. They expected us all to find jobs when we left school and to get married young and start breeding, and they may have reasoned that we would be morally safer making our start in a parish hall exclusively among Catholic girls than to be going to the Astor or Romano's where there would be drinking, fighting and Protestants.

The ceilidh was of its nature exclusively Catholic. If some heroic ecumenists had walked the roads of Andersonstown then to plead with Protestants to come in and meet some nice Catholic young people, they would have found very few living within miles of the school. They would have found none among them any more able to do a ceilidh swing than we were to bowl a cricket ball.

We were complicit in our own spiritual and sexual policing, so strict supervision was hardly necessary. There were some boys who wanted to explore and seek out girls who would let them rummage under their clothing. Most of us, however, thought this was sinful eagerness. Like young pioneers who had sworn off the drink before tasting it, we were nobly disavowing sexual intercourse before the opportunity to enjoy it was even on offer.

In discussions in school and in the Legion of Mary Patrician meetings we imagined ourselves to be perfectly sensible and well able to manage the beast of lust. I remember one strong advocate of disco dancing arguing at a meeting in a packed parish hall that it was the form with the least physical contact. The same man argued that a girl faced with the danger of a cliff-edge rape was entitled to throw herself into the sea and dash her little bones asunder, rather than let a man deprive her of her purity. He had no advice for girls who might find themselves in similar moral danger with no cliff at hand. What if they were being raped in their own living-rooms? Should they try to electrocute themselves in a wall socket or stuff themselves into the fire grate over the burning coals? I wish now I had asked.

At least one sensible girl there stood up and showed how she had been taught to stab a man's eyes out with two fingers. Another explained to a small group afterwards that if you cut an erect penis with a razor blade, the blood would spurt twenty-five feet. She said she always carried a blade for this purpose. Where did they get their good sense from at a time when I was learning so little?

There were always people who were brave enough to be irreverent in the face of religious constraints. In the 1940s, Catholic women used to make rouge for their cheeks by dabbing licked fingers on the cover of the Sacred Heart Messenger, a Jesuit magazine promoting religious devotion.

We, in my generation, postponed our sexual explorations until we could hold out no longer, and then we were confronted with the incompatibility of accepting God's solicitous scrutiny and breaking his laws. Confession was the institutional form of this monitoring by God of our conduct. I can still recall the smell of the dark, polished wood in the confession box. We would join a queue in the pews and wait our turn. We examined our consciences as we did. Then we would enter that musty polished cubicle and face the little grid the priest crouched behind, when the shutter drew back on the smell of boiled cabbage or tobacco on his breath and a large hand shielding his face – and his boredom.

It could be liberating to confess and divest yourself of real guilt. I must have persuaded myself by my teens that the murder of the shrews had not been a sin after all, and that it was a guilt I could, in conscience, keep to myself. It was a relief to have survived confession without crippling shyness or difficult questions. To know that the worst you had done could be erased from the record with the prescribed three Hail Marys was like getting a tax rebate. The sin that simply shamed you, like an act out of character, was easy to be rid of. The trait that was in your character, that kept throwing up the same sins, was more of a problem. It was boring rather than challenging to be going into confession and reporting lies and impure thoughts, as the only sins you could think of, without being very sure that you were guilty of either.

Sex came in as a new category. To be ashamed of it was to be ashamed of your whole being. You were in danger of being corroded by an unsustainable guilt, a guilt at being sexual, which never could be washed away by simply stating the facts of what you had done or by accepting the consolation of prayer. I withheld all mention of sex from confession. When God and sex clashed, the struggle might go on for years, but God was sure to lose.

The tension between religion and sexual development seemed to resolve itself for me suddenly with a spiritual insight. I was fifteen years old and it was the time of the parish mission. For four weeks in Lent the whole running of the parish was given up to the Redemptorist Fathers, all fiery preachers. Every night for those four weeks the church was full. One week was given over to the young people's mission, and Thursday night was reserved for strong language about sex, the big lecture.

A priest gave a blistering sermon reflecting on the pain of the crucifixion. How did we feel, he asked us, about actions of our own which brought this perpetual suffering on Christ who bled and died outside time in the eternal now? Every sin was another thorn through his skull, not a thorn like you find on rose bushes, a huge thorn, six inches long and as hard as iron. Christ was still feeling the thorns driven into his head and those thorns were formed out of our own coarse lasciviousness.

One night in church, I started wondering if all this was complete nonsense. I reasoned thus: if this is all true, and God is real, then nothing else matters, and if God does not exist, then nothing matters anyway. I was going to walk out of that church either a committed follower of Christ or an atheist.

I was not the first or last adolescent to stumble on that do-or-die proposition, but for me that night in church all choice disappeared, and I realised that I would be a priest. My thinking had been intercepted by a fully formed conviction.

I tried out my vocation on a Christmas break at a seminary down the country. Father Murphy, as I'll call him, picked up about six of us at the railway station in Belfast and drove us through the day. It fitted in with my idea of a good break at the time, though it was difficult to orientate myself next day, having arrived in darkness. We were shown the billiard room, where Father Murphy amused the other boys by lifting me up and turning me like a cartwheel. It was the first time anyone had cupped my scrotum, and I was not sure if I had a right to be as displeased as I was.

There was a crypt in the castle grounds and the lead coffins of an old gentleman and his wife had been opened for study. I devised a plan to scare one of the more nervous boys by borrowing one of the coppery skulls and setting it on his pillow as he slept, but the corridors were patrolled at night, and it stayed in my wardrobe, presumably to be discovered later by the cleaner.

My mother thought I would never be a priest because I was too fond of girls. She was right. I liked girls and girls liked me, but now, after this sudden thought about the meaning of life had disturbed me, only fifteen years old and a virgin, I was content to dispense with all sexual interest and commit my life to God. This created problems. My family disapproved, though my parents tolerated the notion for about six months until a priest from a seminary came to clinch the deal. My father said no. I think honestly that was a relief to me. I had carried the weight of my vocation as far as I could. I don't think the Brothers at school ever saw me as a likely priest. But for the six months of my vocation I was a martyr for my faith, especially to my boisterous sister Brid. I would lose every argument when someone, usually her, would say, 'Some priest you are.'

I had given away my right to lose my temper or do anything wrong. I had reinforced the imposition of model behaviour on myself at just the time when I should have been loosening the grasp of religion and entering the mating game. Brid knew that. She could be sentimental and religious too, but as a kind of maudlin reflection on life that she would snap out of into a brasher and truer self. She expected the same of me.

My first girlfriends were Belfast Catholics who were as restrained in how intimate they could be as I was myself. They faced years of struggle between curiosity and fear of God, before they would stand naked with a lover. We were – and this was the word we used – inhibited. Our inhibition would hold us in check when foreplay should have led on to closer touching. Conscience stopped the hands and stilled the lust. At sixteen I was content to lumber a girl for hours without going any further. That way I could feel like a good person.

The first girl who undressed for me was a Protestant. I was hypnotised by the feel of her. Once, I walked her home on a winter's night and dipped my cold hand down her neckline. I nearly strained my wrist winding through her clothes and under her bra, reaching past the curve of her breast to secure her lumpy nipple in my palm. I can't imagine that she enjoyed this, but I presume she was experimenting too. I walked home three miles with the feel of her nipple clenched in my hand, palpably, like a little stone. I concluded that Protestants were more liberal.

Later, a Catholic girlfriend who was religious went off to London on a mission to do charity work with the Legion of Mary and whisked her top off for me on her sofa on her first night home, and let me weigh her loose breasts in my hands. She had discovered that London Catholics could be perfectly devout people without feeling the need to deny themselves. I was more than grateful to them for what they had taught her.

If the Brothers and the parish hadn't made some effort to walk with us part of the way along the road to sexual discovery, they would have lost us earlier. They were dealing with a problem of their own making. You spent ten years in school from the age of five to the age of fifteen with adults who already knew better, trying to tell you that the most profound experience in life is your devout relationship with God. Then one night in your bed you'd try to rub the stiffness out of an intriguing muscle and feel the hot flesh liquify through your fingers. Something happens in your soul. This is new to you. Nothing has prepared you for it. It is profound. You are rethinking the very question of who or what you are. Nothing any teacher or priest has ever said explains it, and you know instinctively that you are not going to ask them. Now we are talking about fundamental autonomous forces.

Finding something in your body which is preordained to work in a certain way raises all the questions about God in nature that occurred to the first people to be stirred by a thunderstorm. You ask yourself: who put that there? What is this power that knows me better than I do myself and lives in my flesh and nerves? I felt like a pagan pilgrim in the woods at night. Now I was alone with the force that moves through all things, and it had my attention.

In those days the religious teachers wanted to delay or suppress that discovery. They wanted the monopoly on mystery. They needed to confine all wonder to a heart filled with devotion, but they weren't very good at that either. I vividly recall a priest at a retreat, when I was sixteen, gyrating with rage at the filthy practice of what he called self-abuse. I was a late developer, despite my loves and kisses, and didn't fully understand what he was on about. But he put me in the mind to try and find out.

The role model we were offered by the Christian Brothers was Matt Talbot, the boy who had the word 'mitcher' beside his name in the old school roll. Matt Talbot, of course, came to no good until his mother's prayers prevailed against fate and he found guilt and God. He died in Dublin in the snow waiting for the church to open. He was found to be mortifying his flesh with chains wrapped under his shirt. Matt never featured in the lectures about self-abuse. No one would have it said about holy Matt Talbot then that he had abused himself.

A Catholic Truth Society pamphlet warned of the danger of

sexual temptation. It said that if you awoke to discover that you were undergoing a 'nocturnal emission', you could trust that you were not sinning, and would not have to confess it, if you didn't indulge the joy of the moment. In other words, as you awoke from an erotic dream, in the hazy moments as you rose to consciousness, as your navel pit filled up with gouts of hot semen, you had to assess the state of your mind, decide whether you were taking pleasure from this (easy question!) and then suppress that pleasure so as not to offend God, who had made it possible in the first place. What were you supposed to do – choke it?

In the view of the Church, no semen, once it had left the man, belonged anywhere but inside a woman and every discharge, even one 'rendered' and accepted for the sake of pure release, had to have a chance of fertilising an egg. If a man's loins stirred, his wife had to open up for him and let chance and God decide if she conceived in doing so.

The Rev. J. E. Mahoney explains all this in his chapter 'Christian Marriage' in George D. Smith's, *The Teaching of the Catholic Church* (1948) ' … if ever a rendering of the debt appears necessary, in order to forestall the danger of incontinence, it is not only lawful but obligatory to pay it, even at the most sacred times.'

The Church was fighting for sperm rights. The sperm must never die in vain. Every one of them was entitled to enter a womb and to have its chance to reach an egg. The horny man, pleading with his tired wife for a shag, was not merely fighting for sexual release; he was, in the Church's view, pleading for the salvation of his immortal soul. A wife's function was to save her husband from sexual incontinence by making herself perpetually available as the only legitimate vessel for his semen.

The celibate priest, who explained this in stilted theological terms did not explain how he and his colleagues were to be spared the sin of incontinence themselves without a woman to resort to.

Years later, Father Oliver Crilly told me that the old CTS pamphlets had come under his control when he headed the Catholic Information Service. He had had them all buried in a landfill site which is now under the road out to the Point Depot in Dublin. That's the right place for them.

A recent sex education video fronted by the Catholic writer, Angela McNamara, takes a more helpful view of wet dreams, describing them as innocent and pleasant but taking the trouble to explain to young girls that they are not the male equivalent of periods. She is a little misleading, however, when she explains that the semen travels *down* through the penis.

I have heard a hundred people say: 'There is nothing wrong with sex. It is a gift from God, to be enjoyed in the proper place and in the proper way.' Three different members of the audience of *The Late Late Show* on RTÉ said it during a discussion on the opening of a sexy lingerie shop in Dublin. But those who speak of sex as a gift always seem to sound as if they would happily give it back. They will say that sex is good, but they mean it in the sense that butter is good; they never seem to believe that sex is enthralling, that it has the power to humble them.

Now I can see that most religion, perhaps all of it, abhors sex. Theologians in all traditions seek to make it functional, to remove the joy from it. This is true of Tibetan tantric practices which depersonalise the woman and extract all emotion from the exchange; it is true of Catholic sexual theology which sees marriage as a contract for the avoidance of sin; and it is also true of clitoridectomy in numerous cultures. Male circumcision among Jews was explained by Moses Maimonides in his *Guide for the Perplexed*: 'The bodily injury caused to that organ is exactly that which is desired; it does not interrupt any vital function, nor does it destroy the power of generation. Circumcision simply counteracts excessive lust ... '

After the Christian Brothers I went to the College of Commerce at Hopefield Avenue in Belfast and mixed with Protestants for the first time. I learned very little about accountancy or the future's markets, but I relaxed. No one there would wave a stick at me. The freedom of this was more important to me than education. This was a disappointment to my new teachers, or lecturers, as we called them, but inevitably I shed all discipline. No one sneered at what I wrote there. I was addressed as Mr O'Doherty, on the presumption that I was an adult. I was going to take time to enjoy this, even if I failed my exams, which I did. Others in the college were indulging themselves in similar ways. One boy used to carve exquisitely defined drawings of an erect penis on the desks. That was the one thing that the principal was always unhinged by.

This was in the last year before the Troubles. I was deciding that I wasn't a Catholic when others were deciding that I had no say in the matter. My rejection of theology was not going to save my life if a Loyalist killer squad got hold of me some night, nor was my free-thinking going to persuade Irish Republican militants that I owed them no allegiance. This Trouble was still a year or two away. I enjoyed the friction between Protestant and Catholic in the college. I was curious about Protestants and they were curious about me.

'Malachi doesn't eat meat on Friday. Go on, have a sausage roll.'

I didn't have a sausage roll, but I realised that conditioning was what held me to abstinence, not faith. One night shortly afterwards, in a bar where I got a part-time job, while making a sandwich for a customer, I folded a slice of roast beef and stuffed it into my mouth. It tasted no worse than it would have done on any other day of the week. That was the end of that abstinence, until I went to India and became a vegetarian. Now every day is an old Catholic Friday for me, with no logic to my eating fish and rejecting meat.

I stopped being a Catholic by degrees. I lost my commitment before I lost my conviction. That is, I gave it up when it clashed with the way I was living my life, before I was really sure I was doing the right thing. But it was so deeply engrained in me that I had to rationalise my way out of it. It wasn't possible simply to give it up like a childhood hobby and turn blithely to something else. The Father in Heaven would want an explanation and I would not be happy until I had worked one out for him. What if I died and went to judgement and couldn't explain to God why I didn't believe in him any more?

I reasoned that it was unnatural to follow a faith which urged me to war on my own nature, that perhaps there was a God, or a life force, but that it was unlikely that my teachers, the Brothers, really knew Him or It any better than, say, the Protestants I met at college. The wider the circle I moved in, the more open the question became, and the more free I felt to seek my own answer in my own good time.

One of the strangest aspects for me of the story of what happened in Catholic Belfast in 1970, when I was nineteen, was that the same boys who had rejected the discipline of the Brothers in school, assimilated the Brothers' values from the traditionalists of the Provisional IRA who led them into war. The teachers went to visit these boys in the jails: the boys who had smoked in the sheds, who had mitched school, who had copied their homework and cheated in exams, the spirited ones who were not conned. And what did they find? They found them saying the rosary in Irish in their cells and singing together in the evening the little Irish language songs that they had refused to learn at school.

The ones who joined the Provisionals were the ones the Christian Brothers had made least impression on at school. Many went on to become, belatedly, exemplary Brothers' boys, by this alternative route. Those of us who completed the course with the Brothers, and didn't fight them, came to laugh at the early indoctrination. We could see through it. It was the ones who fought it who fell for it in the end. Why? Just, I suppose, because it was restated to them by the men who wanted to arm them and send them out to kill soldiers. Where revolutionaries in other countries were enthused by new ideas and dreams of social reform, ours consulted their parents and teachers on what to believe. In asserting the right not to be demeaned for being Irish and Catholic, they gave new life to their old conservative ways.

The Brothers were actually more flexible than this suggests. They liked to make space for you to know them as men, so they softened everything for you when you were older and tried to include you in the joke. If you had already left with a grudge and a wounded spirit, you missed that part of the message.

Suddenly the sky had darkened and I was afraid of being killed or arrested. I had nightmares about being caught by the sinister Captain Black, who claimed responsibility for murders of Catholics on behalf of the Ulster Defence Association. I also had anxiety dreams about being arrested by the army and found to have a gun in my possession. I am aware of what a Freudian would make of those gun dreams, but the reality is that many of my neighbours were caught with guns and jailed. There were guns all around us.

Once I attracted the army to raiding our house through my drunken stupidity, but I was brave enough to take responsibility. My father had come into the bedroom to say that soldiers were in the garden below. I opened the window and blew a whistle. This was the standard warning to people around us that soldiers were about. I wasn't intending to warn anybody, just being reckless to see what would happen. I had even bought the whistle to be ready for such a moment, which must say something about the state of my mind. The mischief was premeditated but ill-considered.

There was a thud then which I thought at first was a shot from a rubber bullet gun. I stood silently with my father on the landing listening for more before I realised that someone was kicking in the back door. My mother went to the head of the stairs. An enormous soldier with a rifle stepped into the living-room and looked up at us. All life's consequences had come at once. I pushed to the front of the frightened family group on the stairs. The soldier wrenched my collar with one hand and lifted me, as if it was easier for him to bring my face level with his that way than by bending down. Men like him didn't bend. He smelled of damp cotton and oil and sweat. My mother was standing there in a pink night-dress, not knowing what was happening. She was shrieking at him. He had scattered a tray stand that she had placed by the door. This was not anybody's home as far as this man was concerned. He had no more regard for our living-room than he would have had for a public toilet. He dragged me out to his men and stood me against the wall. He pointed his rifle at me.

'I am going to shoot you, Paddy.'

I reasoned that if a bullet passed through me it might go into the house and hurt someone. By treating this as an intellectual exercise, I was holding back the tide of shame that would accuse me, rightly, of having brought this to our home. 'Not here,' I said. He didn't like that. I don't know why he was exasperated; perhaps because he had not intended me to really believe that he would shoot me. Perhaps he hoped I would run so that he could more easily justify shooting me. His men were standing around watching to see how he would finish what he had started. Exasperated, he turned his gun away and grabbed my shirt and dragged me behind him, through the garden. After a few yards, he threw me down and kicked me in the face. I felt nothing. We ploughed through the garden hedge, scratching the thick oily cotton of his uniform and my skin. Still I felt nothing. This didn't count, I thought, because far worse was to come. I wondered if I would still feel nothing then.

When we reached their Pig, their Armoured Personnel Carrier, the soldier made me stand with my fingertips against the metal wall. He loosened a chain from the underside of the vehicle and dropped it to the ground where a multicoloured flame hissed a moment.

'Are you in the IRA?'

'Who is in the IRA?'

His questions were stupid. I felt the faint tingle of electric current in my fingers and body. The men were curious, looking at me. Last year I touched a farmer's live wire fence with the tips of my fingers and recalled that same tingle, but the real shock was a blow to the small of my back like a firm punch. I had felt nothing like it from the shocks the soldiers gave me. One of them noticed that my fingers lapped through the shutter of the vehicle and that he could close the shutter on me and guillotine them. That's what he did. He held the lever that angled back from the shutter and drew it tight over one finger. He could have broken bone, but he changed his mind and stopped, opened the shutter again, and just sat there watching me. Maybe he thought the sight of me being electrocuted would be more fun. Maybe, like the one with the gun, he simply couldn't muster the resolve to damage someone so totally available to him. I wondered then about the crucifixion and realised that Christ had felt nothing. The whole story had a different meaning now.

The soldier in charge pointed either his baton or a rubber bullet gun at me. 'You're going to get it.'

Get what? They just puzzled me, these people. The tingles through my body continued at intervals of a few seconds. I could not believe they expected these to impress me. They were nothing. Nothing they did could have demoralised me like Kipperhead calling me a fool. Physically they could have destroyed me. I had been living in the fear that someone would some day physically destroy me, but this was like a contest between two obtuse forces, the stupidity of their fumbling for a way to enjoy having me under their power, and the refusal or inability of my body to comprehend or feel what was happening. I had already learned the reflex of detaching myself from terror.

I would probably have respected them more if they had succeeded in making me panic. Part of me wanted to be over-awed.

Sooner or later the pain would get strong enough to hold my attention. Then, perhaps because they had lost interest, perhaps because they didn't really know what they were doing, the soldiers let me go. They just didn't have enough commitment to breaking me. They did not have the passion or the faith of a Kipperhead.

'You're a terrorist,' said Stephen, a journalist I worked with then. 'You terrorised them. They were crapping themselves as much as you were.'

I left Belfast in 1972, after the horror of the first three years of trouble. The manly men were in control, and I had had enough of that already. 'There's going to be changes round here,' my father had often shouted. He never changed. In his eighties, when I was fifty, I was visiting him at home and he was scowling at the television. 'Will you fucking look at that? Does anybody put as much cheese as that on a biscuit? I don't know. They think we're fucking stupid.'

PART TWO

*'Jay-ay Guroo-oo Day-va. Jay-ay Guroo-oo Day-va.'*
   *I had absorbed something of the language and music and religious culture of India before ever going there or meeting an Indian person. It was on the stereo in the corner and in the books that were around me. None of this was based much on the actual India, but in the reflections of hippy meditators and acidheads, George Harrison and Timothy O'Leary. A blue-jean trail had been opened up to the ashrams of Rishikesh and Hardwar in days when Iran and Afghanistan were passable by bus, usually a bus with a cannabis plant painted on the side of it. We imagined India to be the most peaceful place on earth, the perfect place to get stoned. So I had thought of going to India before the opportunity arrived, and I had enough job-lot theology in my head to be able to imagine that the opportunity itself, when it arrived, was proof of destiny.*

I was young and knew very little but thought I knew a lot. After a start in journalism on a Sunday paper in Belfast in the worst year of the Troubles, I grabbed a lifeline that took me to the north of England. I met Linda when hitch-hiking to Amsterdam from Belfast. She was eighteen and travelling in the same direction from Lancaster. It was the longest and best lift I ever got. She was skinny and wore mini dresses and was a couple of inches taller than me. She spoke with a soft and husky Lancashire accent. She walked with a lilt and her face seemed always to be shaking itself free of her blonde hair to find me when we talked, like a cat nosing out from behind a curtain. It simply surprised me that she liked me.

She was lighter than me. She did not have the shadow of fear across her that I had acquired in Belfast, nor did she live with the sort of perpetual fret that was in me about politics, God or self-respect. She had not even been christened as a child. She would look back at my dark gaze and simply wish that I would relax; I would look at her frivolity and ease and feel an urge to explain Belfast, Catholicism and Irishness. She would say: 'Maybe I should not go out with an Irishman. Maybe they are just too different.'

She was thinking: 'If you need me to be as fucked up as you are, then maybe I should find someone else.'

I needed the security of the relationship, yet I was always testing it. 'Who do you love?' I'd say every day.

I learned a few new things: how to hitch-hike round England, how to inhale the smoke of cannabis and how to enter the soft fixity it takes the smoker into. I became a contemplative of sorts then. One evening Linda's brother, Steve, stopped his car just to look at the sunset over Morecambe Bay. I wondered for a moment if he was crazy. Then I decided that it cost nothing to enjoy this moment. Then we went for a pint. Smoking cannabis slowed the mind down to take time to look and listen and changed the texture of experience. It slowed it enough to enable you to watch a joke forming in your mind. Was it an illusion that we enjoyed paradoxes too complex even to articulate?

I pushed Linda away when I felt she needed me, and I needed her when I did not have her. After one of the break-ups, when she had moved to Hull University, and I had followed her, I took a cheap and dingy bedsit flat and discovered in less than one day there that I was a baby desperate for intimacy and comfort. I was not ready to be alone and independent. I was living on just a film over terror. I was screaming for the breast.

I will not lightly forget the desperation of loneliness, the howl in the heart for something to happen now, right now, and the gasp of horror at it not happening. You pray when you are in that state. Your whole being pleads with the indefinable unknowable beyond you, and you don't huff and refuse to deal with it until it has identified itself to your agnostic intellect.

I was twenty-three and desperately lonely, and though I screamed out for human contact and went into pubs to talk to people who were too distracted to talk to me, I knew that my own evident loneliness and the urgency of meeting people was making me unattractive to those I was pitching myself at. Part of me understood what the solution was, what the appropriate prayer was, if you like, and it was not, 'Send me a friend God', but 'Help me learn to live with this'.

Some very strange things happened at that time. One night I had slept on the floor of a half-friend at the university. I woke in the morning in my sleeping bag and lit a cigarette. I watched

Martin in the bed. He murmured, then he seemed to hear me, or hear something, and he sat up. He had a big broad naked chest. He looked straight ahead calmly, and then started fretting, and then screaming. He was in terror of something approaching him, something invisible to me. The fright of this woke me up – again. It had been a dream.

That left me in a bewildered state for hours. It was the first time I thought that there was a genuine puzzle in Chuang Tzu's reflections on a butterfly. I was reading late T'ang poetry and scraps of mystical writings then. Chuang Tzu had dreamt that he was a butterfly, then wondered when he woke if he was a butterfly dreaming that he was Chuang Tzu. Only when dreaming was indistinguishable from the waking state might someone doubt reality, but it had been.

That afternoon I sat in the bay window of the living-room of the house I lived in, in Margaret Street. Suddenly an army lorry pulled up, accompanied by the green Austin 1800s officers travelled in. This was Hull, not Belfast. Armed soldiers leapt out of the lorry, ran the length of the street and sealed off both ends. I watched them raid an empty house in a block across from me. I questioned in my own mind whether this was really happening at all. It was an army exercise.

My morale improved in the summer of 1975 after a series of disasters forced me to toughen up in manageable stages. I was back living in Lancaster, though I travelled most weeks across the Pennines to visit Linda in Hull. The house that I lived in was raided while I wasn't home, by both the drugs squad and the Special Branch, so I moved out. I had heard from others that Irish people were being stitched up by the police on bombing charges, and I didn't want to be another of them. Looking back now, it seems even more likely than I thought then that I could have been nailed in that way. I have questions about a man who came to our house with a friend, showed us all an old rusty pistol and passed it around. I left my fingerprints on that gun, perhaps as evidence for a local detective to use if he needed more arrests.

I took a summer job on a farm in Worcester, picking hops and then apples, and by the autumn I had saved some money. I was also physically fitter, and more confident of myself, having camped in fields for a couple of months and spent glorious summer evenings cooking my meals in the shade of a fallen elm, looking out towards the Welsh hills. That experience gave me the courage to move when the opportunity arose. It came in the form of an advertisement in the personal column of *The Guardian*: 'Retired author required to work with Swami in India on idealistic commentary on *Bhagavad Gita*.'

I answered the ad, though I was an unemployed journalist, not a 'retired author'. It had been placed by Walter Hartmann, a German economics professor who was a disciple of Swami Paramananda Saraswati. He wrote me an effusive letter telling me that he sensed that I was the right person for the job and asking me to phone him to make the arrangements. Hartmann was full of giddy enthusiasm and told me that it would not only be an education for me but would lead to my becoming an enlightened yogi. 'An enlightened yogi has realised the Self of all things in his own self,' he said. 'He has found God.'

Hartmann was practising meditation under the guidance of Swamiji and teaching it in Germany and Austria. He had for years been a follower of Maharishi Mahesh Yogi and taught his system of Transcendental Meditation but now believed Swamiji's teaching to be the more authentic.

He sent me a photograph of Swamiji, a bullish man of forty or fifty, with shoulder-length black hair and a greying black beard. He was sitting wrapped in a length of saffron silk, and he looked powerful and daunting. 'The people in India worship him as God.'

I would meet Swamiji two months later.

On a December morning in 1975, with a slight hangover, I kissed Linda goodbye on her doorstep in Hull, not knowing if we were parting for good or not, and walked with my rucksack to the railway station. I had to lift each foot with deliberation, order myself to take each step and suppress the impulse to turn round. The train trundled to London. I met a man who told me he had lived in India as a child and advised me to eat only Kwality ice cream when I got there. He offered me space on his hotel bedroom floor. Trusting a stranger seemed a bad way to start a long journey. I slept on a seat in Heathrow. The clouds over Saudi Arabia looked like wafer, almost on the ground. India itself looked sparse and bare. The urge to rush home was strongest now, but it was too late. The Delhi air was as hot as summer in Ireland and there was a reassuring smell, familiar from childhood. That was it – coalsmoke.

Swamiji's full title and name were Balyogi shree Swami Para-mananda Sarswati ji Maharaj. The title balyogi was a boast that he had never had sex. He would be a parent figure to me for the next three years, and even which parent, I can't easily say. He was a gruff man who responded to others only when he wished to, and often left those around him disconcerted by his apparent indifference to them. That was the difficult part for me, wondering if mannerisms I took to mean one thing at home meant the same in him, if his detachment was arrogant contempt for me or a spiritual remove.

He was proud to have been born a *brahmin*, a member of the priest caste, and he carried the sacred thread of the *brahmin* wrapped round his staff, with the whole staff sheathed in saffron cotton. Having become a monk, or *sannyasin*, that is, one who renounces the world and pledges himself to celibacy and poverty, he believed he had ceased to be a *brahmin* too, but he still carried the sign that he had been one, and expected greater respect on account of that. He also drew attention to the fact that he had two MAs.

He had been discovered as a man of spiritual potential by Swami Brahmananda Saraswati, who had been the guru of Maharishi Mahesh Yogi, the man famed for teaching Transcendental Meditation in Europe. Swamiji and Mahesh were, therefore, guru brothers. In a way, that makes guru cousins of me and George Harrison. Brahmananda held the title *Shankaracharya* or guardian of the teachings of the ancient sage, Shankara. There are four of these in India, in the North, South, East and West. He was the northern one, based at Jyotirmath. Shankara had taught a system of logic by which one could realise that God was one and indivisible and that nothing else really existed. Shankara taught that all souls, aspiring to happiness, actually aspired to God. This philosophy is called the *Advaita Vedanta*.

At first, I stayed with Swamiji at a pilgrim hostel or *dharamshala* by the Ganges in a little town called Brig Ghat. On the first morning I went to work with him there, Mr Dikchit, who was supervising construction work on a new ashram for him there, rehearsed me in the proper reverential greeting, '*Namo Narayanay*'. This means, though Mr Dickcit did not have enough English to translate it for me: 'I bow to the living God'. I forgot the phrase in seconds. I approached Swamiji, sitting in his cane chair, with his books and files on the table beside him, and said instead: 'Good morning.'

He drew attention to my failure in a manner that I would become familiar with, effecting to treat it simply as a matter of academic interest. 'Yes, I understand that that is a respectful form of greeting in your country, and that the reply is, Good Morning.'

'Yes,' I said.

'And, I believe some people say, How do you do? And the answer to that is, How do you do?'

I did not voice my own cynical thought: that I might prostrate myself to him, if he would prostrate himself to me.

I learned early that Swamiji was not a man you would want to share your table with at a business lunch. If you were trying to keep your credibility among professional associates, and particularly among some in my own sceptical profession, journalism, you would not defer to a man who had such a strange view of the world as he had.

He didn't have to care what other people thought of him for he knew their role in life was to look up to him. He probably had no idea that those who loved him, occasionally joked about him. Their private mockery of his little ways had no effect on him. There was no joke for him, or for anyone else as he saw it, in his decision to perm his hair. He had made a resolve, as part of his adoption of the vow of *Sanyasa*, not to cut it. Every *sadhu* or monk makes some decision about hair. Some have their heads shaved regularly, some simply let the hair grow. Swamiji, who could not bear to have strangers touch him, let his grow. In old photographs he is just a mop of black curly hair. The camera might as well have been pointed at the back of his head as at the front. Hartmann, suggested a perm. He brought perming tongs from Germany, and Swamiji's mop was folded back to uncover his face, which was good, because he had powerful engaging eyes.

We established a routine. Each evening we would walk out onto the main road that runs over the Ganges, but turn away from the river and out along a long straight country road through the cane fields. We walked side by side, sometimes content not to talk. I would take care not to brush against him, because he followed, and taught, the rule of 'untouchability'. This forebade physical contact with people of lower castes and those of no caste, like myself.

I later had the courage to challenge him to explain this to me. He said only that devout people should avoid physical contact with others, because all sin began with touch. He never simply owned up to perpetuating a tradition which might be offensive, and which had caused great pain to people of the untouchable castes. He was adamant that there were sound, spiritual reasons for untouchability, regardless of the offence implied. 'Believe me, if your life is at stake and you need my hand, you shall have it,' he said grandly.

I taunted him and said: 'But we are breathing the same air. The fly that lands on me, moves on and lands on you.'

His face contorted with disgust. I noticed once that when I brushed against his strap underwear on the clothesline, he sent Mrs Chauhan, the wife of his ashram manager, to take it down and wash it again, yet he would stand sometimes stroking the arch of a buffalo's neck and not realise that he was telling me by his action that I was dirtier than a beast.

In the beginning, it was simply too much trouble to assert my independence. I could have refused to live in the little stone room in the *dharamshala* and insisted on going to restaurants and eating meat; or demanded more money for my own use, and simply rebuffed his assumption of authority, but it would all have been a struggle, and the only hand I had to play was that I could leave if I wasn't happy. He would always expect me to be available for work or conversation, and when I went out, I knew that I would have to tell him where I had been. It was easier to go along with his ways and procrastinate day by day on my declaration of autonomy. What point was there in contending with him when he and his people were the only friends I now had?

Brig Ghat existed only to serve pilgrims and had a listless look when there were none about. The large *dharamshalas* stood empty. The proprietors of the little thatched tea shops dozed on low, strung cots called *charpois* but kept their fires burning just in case someone did come along. Often I came along, sat on a bench and made scanty conversation with them as they fanned their fires, mixed tea, milk and sugar in the same pot and served it in throwaway earthenware mugs like misshapen flowerpots that wouldn't stand on a level surface and whose remains littered the streets like red gravel.

Though only a couple of hours east of Delhi, this was a part of India few tourists saw. I was a novelty there. I met people who had never encountered English and who thought they could make themselves understood better by simply shouting the same Hindi words louder at me. I attracted crowds around me when I walked out. Students come to bathe, would confront me directly in the bazaar with hands offered for shaking and they would say: 'What is your name? Where are you coming from? What is your qualification?' Once a crowd of ten surged at me and I thought I was about to be beaten up, but they were just curious.

The ear had to acclimatise to India as much as had the eye. Vendors rang brass bells to advertise their goods. Marriage parties paraded in the evening, led by brass bands and even by men with shotguns, firing into the air. A rickshaw fitted with a record player and a loudspeaker would come to town to advertise the films being shown in Hapur or Meerut. Cars on the main highway honked their horns as they approached the town to warn cyclists and pedestrians, or just to let the car in front know that they intended overtaking. That was the local driving style. Swamiji and the others thought that this was a quiet town, but my impression was that there was a madness in it.

Those who knocked at my door, Raj Pal, the 'boy' who looked after the *dharamshala*, or others, would knock incessantly until they got an answer. Swamiji himself often made his presence felt by noise, by the clumping of his sandals and by his habit of clearing his throat with a loud ringing 'Gha-Heeeee!' This was a yoga exercise called *Rechak*, he told me. It produces a refreshing shudder. And when I heard him scolding the cook or one of the workmen he shrieked until the air was charged with his displeasure and no one around him could be at ease.

This abolished my notions of the Indian love of tranquillity. On top of the noise of the people was the braying of donkeys, the clatter of small workshops and the trundling of trains on the iron bridge. I could have brought back a wealth of impressions of the place, even if I had been blind. And in this noisy town, the sale of eggs in the shops was forbidden as it would have violated the religious purity of the place. Nobody worried that the noise did as much.

Cleanliness was a higher spiritual value than silence, and sometimes it meant more than hygiene. Eggs, for instance, were thought of as dirty food. No amount of cleaning and boiling them would have made them any cleaner to the mind of Swamiji than they were when they emerged from a hen's grimy orifice.

On the day before the January full moon, pilgrims began to flock into Brig Ghat. Men set up new stalls in the bazaar, selling drums, charms and blankets. Fortune-tellers and beggars, some of them grotesquely deformed, lined the way to the riverbank and the ghat. I had been walking with Swamiji in the evening. We hadn't been speaking. At first on our walks I questioned him about his faith. My questions had become superfluous anyway in the face of his predictable answers. One of these was: 'You will understand the truth of this from your own spiritual experience later on.'

Instead of taking our usual shortcut off the main road and round the back of the market place, we walked as far as the bridge and descended the steps there to the edge of the river. It was dark and a glorious moon was rising. I would get to know the moon there, from sleeping on rooftops and waking through the night in the hot seasons. People say there is a face in the moon. Others see a hare. I have found three different faces from different perspectives, and the hare too. Around us, on undulating barren waste ground, groups of people gathered by campfires and still pillars of smoke rose in the cool air. The water was silent but for a slight lapping. I looked out and saw the arch of a huge dark fish slice out and back like a deft secret. A funeral pyre was burning fiercely on a sandbar in the middle of the river.

'Do you like this scene?' Swamiji asked.

'Yes. I do.'

He stopped and stood with his hands behind his back, drawing the woollen shawl neatly around him. 'There is activity, and yet it is peaceful.'

In the morning I walked alone out over the bridge and stopped to watch the sun rise. Luminescent pale red seeped across the sky and water, from the same point at which the moon had emerged the night before. Thousands of pilgrims stood on the bank and about a hundred stood in the river praying, isolated from each other and from the crowd behind them by their concentration.

Throughout that day I found it hard to recognise my Brig

Ghat. I hadn't been there long but I had become possessive of it. All the rooms in the *dharamshala* and in all the *dharamshalas* were taken. From the first floor of ours, a dozen wet saris hung into the courtyard. The streets were so tightly packed with people that it was difficult to move. Fingerless lepers held out shrivelled palms for coins. The smell was oppressive: old cotton and shit.

Later that day Mr Dikchit, who was supervising the ashram construction, invited me to go down to the Ganges to bathe. We walked down the street and across the sand to the edge of the river. We found a shallow part, away from where the crowd was dense. A man came over to me and put some granules of sugar into my hand.

'*Prasad*,' he said.

I accepted it and handed it to Dikchit.

'*Prasad*,' I said.

*Prasad* is sacrifice. Like the eucharist, it is offered to God, sanctified by that offering and then distributed to worshippers and guests or even to passers-by. Dikchit did not accept the sugar from me. I didn't know why. I didn't know yet that I was 'untouchable'. I put some of the sugar in my pocket to throw to the birds later on. I undressed and waded into the water in a pair of bathing trunks, the smartest pair on the riverbank that day. Most of the other men wore striped pyjama shorts or their *dhotis* and the women wore saris.

I felt absurdly tall when, on my knees, the water did not reach my waist.

Throughout the afternoon I was an object of curiosity. People came to my door to watch me; and study my movements. They examined the western artefacts, the typewriter, the carbon paper and the toilet paper. They wanted to feed me. 'Please accept. It is our religion to feed a guest.'

Yet I felt that these people who were, ostensibly, offering so much were really trying to take something away from me, if only some tale of my companionship that they could later pass on to their neighbours.

In the first months, I missed Linda, almost as if she had been pulled out of me. Some nights, I stood by the river looking at the moon and working out at what angle it would sit in the sky from the window through which she could see it too. I had to try and reason with the panic to be with her. It would take at least a week to get to her, so why not endure a week more, then perhaps another?

At that time Swamiji had workers laying the foundations of the ashram he was building beside the main road out of town. He would inspect the site in the evenings, and then we would take our evening walk out along the narrow road. I would have him to myself and I let him see how curious I was about meditation. 'People will say of someone who gives his life to it that he is wasting his time, cutting himself off from the world?'

I felt guilty about not having newspapers there. I was not keeping track of the murders at home and I did not know that there was civil war in Angola. This also was the time of Indira Gandhi's dictatorial rule, the Emergency, and I had no idea what effect it was having.

'On the contrary,' said Swamiji, 'there is no greater challenge for a man than that he control his mind.'

'What is the difference between meditation and prayer?'

'Meditation is the highest form of prayer. In the spiritual state of *samadhi*, which follows from meditation, there is no distinction between the soul and God, but both are one.'

The other problem was sex, not just that I was not getting any, but that if I followed Swamiji's advice I never would again. He insisted that meditation required sexual abstinence, 'Because semen is the food of your brain.'

He said I would understand this if I had sexual intercourse every day for two weeks, and suffered the inevitable mental depletion consequent on that. I said I thought I had already passed that test without appreciable damage. He rounded on me, appalled. I also mocked his determination to assert that he knew more about most things than science taught, particularly his version of what causes eclipses of the moon. He said it was the serpent Rahu attacking it. I wondered then how science could predict the actual moment at which Rahu would do this. He said: 'The materialists cannot give up their ideas about the sun and the moon. How else are they to explain night and day?'

How indeed?

Swamiji lived the ascetic life. He drank every day from the water of the Ganges, which he regarded as holy. He believed that it was always clean, no matter how dirty it looked. If he was not living beside the Ganges, as he did for much of the year, he had water from the river brought to him. I had hoped at first that the mystical faith he propounded, ruled out the anthropomorphic religion that regarded the river as a Goddess, but it didn't.

'These things have been proven scientifically,' he would insist. Science was a worry. He would always feel safer with his arguments if he could persuade himself that they were scientifically validated, but if science went against them, it was because it was arrogant, materialistic and in no way a valid guide to the truth about anything. He argued that theories of heredity confirmed the value of the *Varna* system which divided Hindu society into four distinct classes: the *Brahmin* priests, the *Kshatriya* warriors, the *Vaishya* merchants and the *Sudra* labourers. It matches the division of society in the suits of the Tarot cards, the cups, swords, coins and staves. Then there were the aliens, outside the system itself, the Indian *Dalet* people whom Gandhi had called the *Harijans*, or children of God, and foreigners like myself.

'The west would redeem this system themselves if they could, for they are beginning to see the value of it,' said Swamiji. I said I had not heard anywhere that they were.

When people visited Swamiji they bowed low before him, often touched his feet (if their caste status allowed them to) and greeted him with the words Dikchit had tried to teach me, *Namo Narayanay*, I bow to the living God. He did nothing to correct them if he thought he wasn't the living God. At the start of the monsoon, when he entered a period of confinement by rivers, his followers would celebrate the Guru Puja. They would perform an act of worship before him, offering sweetmeats and flower petals at his feet. They would hold the brass tray of offerings and the burning incense and move it in circles before him as they sang the prayers of obeisance, as if he was a breathing icon.

We had numerous arguments about the incarnation of God. I simply refused to believe that God came down on earth and mingled as a human being. I had my mind made up on that.

'Your mind is closed,' he would say. I changed my argument to a more agnostic one. I would say: 'OK, maybe God did that, and maybe God didn't, but I cannot know that.'

'You can, if you listen and open your heart,' he said.

I said to him one day when we were taking our evening walk:

'Do you not think it a pity that a lot of people are distracted from the *Gita* by its support for the *Varna* system?'

'The pity is that people do not always recognise a good thing.'

I realised that if I was to make any progress in my relationship with him I would have to avoid this subject in particular.

'Well, do you think it is possible for someone to accept part of the *Gita* while rejecting the rest?'

'Oh yes.' He was leaving that avenue open to me. 'If one accepts a small part of the truth and loves it, that truth will grow and the time will come when he will be able to accept the rest. At least, if he recognises that the *Gita* contains wisdom, he should be more receptive to the things in it which are harder to grasp, than if he had heard those things from the mouth of a fool.'

One day we were out walking and I directed the conversation towards his spiritual beliefs. He stopped and invited me to sit down. 'We start with a question: Who are you? Are you the empirical reality which your senses perceive? No, then work back from there to see what you are. Are you your body?'

The question seemed a silly one. 'No, I am not my body.'

'Are you the senses that perceive the body and the world? Is the real self to be located there?'

I thought about that for a while and agreed that I wasn't to be identified with my eyes and ears and taste buds, but that these served something else.

'Then is it the mind that is the self?'

I conceived of the mind as the whole mental being, most of it unconscious. He defined it as the effervescent pool of impressions and ideas which would become wholly transparent, and cease to distract the self, if all thought could stop and all senses be withdrawn, like the limbs of a tortoise into its shell.

'You must shut out the sense impressions, forget the body and curtail all impulses of desire and fear, still all query, go beyond the intellect and transcend all that is not you. Then you will find the answer.'

I closed my eyes there and looked into dark space with a mind that was clear of any thought for a moment other than its own determination to see through itself. It was still the me I always knew. In the scriptures, he told me, the Ultimate Reality, or God, is called Sat Chit Ananda, Being, Consciousness and Bliss, because all that can be surmised about it is that it is, that it is conscious and that it is content. The individual self is an illusion, like a wave on the sea imagining itself separate from the whole sea.

'If God is joy, if God is good, why is there pain and suffering in the world. Surely God is to blame for this?' I asked. And at the same time, I wasn't seriously expecting an answer because I didn't believe that he or anyone could answer it.

'Think of God as the Sun. It shines evenly on everything, yet some things wilt and some things thrive. Do you blame the Sun for this?'

He could have used a gospel metaphor there: Do you blame the earth because the seed that falls on barren ground does not grow?

'Why do you talk of God as a person and also in impersonal terms as Being, Consciousness and Bliss?'

'God is everything. You can think of Him as a tree if it suits you. You can gather water in a vessel of any shape, or you can drink directly from the pool, or even immerse yourself. It is still water, shapeless, perpetual.'

None of this was Swamiji's own individual message; what he taught was the traditional *Advaita Vedanta* from the sage Shankara. He would have been angered by any suggestion that he had changed it. All of it was available from books already. Much of what he taught about stilling the mind by focusing it on God was similar also to teachings in Christian literature like *The Cloud of Unknowing*, or St Teresa of Avila's *Interior Castle*. He offered himself as the bearer of tradition, not of a radical or personal interpretation. He was orthodox; which meant that he spoke words he had been reciting, like any other clergy-person, in the same form and order for decades. He had an answer for everything.

The topic that we discussed most frequently was reincarnation and he would say: 'Well think carefully about it and look for the truth in my words.'

He often said things like that to coax me into a receptive rather than a critical state of mind. 'You were born into a family with other children. You inherited, like them, certain characteristics, yet you have individual traits, and very early in life you displayed a personality which was all your own. Where did those individual traits come from? Just from heredity?

'Karma means action. Actions condition the intellect. The intellect at the time of dying is one-pointed in the form of the greatest desire in the heart, normally for a certain kind of life. That soul will go to a body which will seek to fulfil that desire. The seeker of truth will arrive at circumstances conducive to the continuation of that search. One whose actions have reduced him to the level of a beast, will arrive at circumstances conducive to the enjoyment of his bestiality.'

'So experience trains us to want God?'

'No. Desire grows by what it feeds on and may carry a man deeper into the depths of depravity and indulgence.'

Swamiji never saw any reason to qualify his words to include women. Women, he believed, were spiritually lower than men. His arguments in defence of this were drawn only from his own Hindu culture. 'A son is a blessing to a family and a daughter is a burden. You raise her to adulthood only to have her serve another family, but a son stays with you and supports you till you die.'

It would have meant little to argue that society could arrange itself differently. He had no wish to see Hindu society change.

'Has my karma brought me here to India?' I asked.

'There can be no doubt about it. How many times have you died, like all men, disgusted with the futility and hollowness of the lives you have lived? At last you turned to yearning for the peace that comes with wisdom, and that yearning has brought you here.'

Soon all our discussions were about meditation.

'The first thing,' he said, 'is learning to concentrate. You think you are the master of your thoughts, but if you close your eyes and try to keep your mind blank, you will soon realise that they are the master of you.'

He was right. We don't choose what to think or when to think. Thought is automatic and persistent.

'But surely people who don't think are zombies?'

'The world is already full of zombies because people's minds are full of rubbish.'

By the Ganges I could imagine that we were in a virtual paradise, but when we walked together by the Jamuna River in Delhi a few weeks later it seemed an absurd privilege to be able to discuss the meaning of life among people who were living in squalor. On a raised embankment stood hundreds of low huts of mud and straw. The people there were dressed in ragged and dirty clothes. They were sitting or working or queuing at the water pump. Nearly every hut had a rickshaw outside. No one works harder than the driver of a cycle rickshaw, and this was what they got for their efforts. Along one side of the embankment were little piles of stinking shit. Below the embankment were small vegetable allotments. Beyond, tall chimneys belched thick black smoke. Swamiji held a saffron handkerchief to his nose without any polite effort to mask his revulsion. A girl in blackened rags ran up to me and held out her hand. 'Baksheesh! Baksheesh!' I knew that if I gave her money I would soon have dozens of others round me – it had happened before – so I gave her nothing.

'Baksheesh, Sahib. Baksheesh!'

Swamiji barked at her and she left us alone. Farther along a woman joined us. She had a naked baby on her hip.

'Baksheesh,' she said. She raised her fingers to her mouth.

'Baksheesh!' She tugged her bodice away from her breasts to show how lean and wizened they were, and she put one breast in the mouth of the baby.

'Baksheesh! Baksheesh!'

I ignored her relentlessly. There was a park at the end of the embankment. We followed a path past a group of boys who were flying little square fighter kites. Swamiji explained that the kite strings were coated with ground glass and that each boy was trying to cut the string of the other. We climbed a hill and I could see greenery and tailored flower beds around us. This was *Shantivan*, the forest of peace, prepared in commemoration of India's first Prime Minister, Jawaharlal Nehru.

'We can sit here, if you like,' said Swamiji. I agreed, and we sat down like lords of the land below us. But I now had a question.

'What do you really mean when you say that the world is unreal?'

He took me again through the stages of his philosophy, but I doubted at the end of it I would be left with anything that would equip me for the embarrassment of having to shrug off destitute beggars.

'If you anticipate liberation from the world, then you must act in the world in such a way that your heart will be purified. Refine your instinct and free it of boisterous and cynical impulses. This law compels you to be compassionate and gentle. So love these people. See God in them. You will come closer to an understanding that we are all one if you act in this world as if you are losing nothing by giving and gaining nothing by taking.'

'But why are they in that condition?'

'The *Gita* says: "All things are born of action in this world of men." They are paying the price of past deeds.'

'And so, if they are getting what they deserve, do you think we may contentedly leave them to it?'

'Yes, but then you will lose an opportunity to act for the purification of your own lower nature.'

He seemed to be saying that the poor were there for the rest of us to practise our virtues on, or not, as we pleased.

One day we were walking together out to the riverside park. We had been discussing the New Testament and Swamiji had said that he would show me a perspective on it that I had not had before. He invited me to read it and then present him with questions. On the way to the park we passed a woman who was lying by the side of the road in the shade of a high wall. She was skeletal and she was groaning. She could not move. Her clothes were in disarray. I looked at her and swore. 'My Christ, look. Isn't that lovely?'

'I see you have some irony in you.' Swamiji sounded as if he had just learned the word 'irony' the day before and was trying it out.

'I thought you would have known that by now.'

'Perhaps it is a quality in all men of your race. I have read it is so.'

Maybe he felt I was sneering at India and so he was jibing at Ireland in return.

'Perhaps it is.'

A beggar passed close to us with a pan in his hand and I, feeling uneasy about not taking responsibility for the woman, gave him all the coins I had. But Swamiji had not eased his step so I had to trot to catch up with him.

We sat in the park by the river.

'Now what are your questions?'

'I have no questions.'

'Very well. I thought you had wanted my help in understanding the Bible, but it seems that I have been wasting my time.'

'I'm sorry if you feel that. I think I understand the Gospels well enough.'

We walked back. I parted with him when we reached the road and walked to Kashmiri Gate to a bookshop. I tried to concentrate on books to persuade myself that I wasn't fretting about the woman dying by the roadside. If I admitted that, I would have to take action, and I didn't know what action to take. I was afraid that if I helped one starving beggar I would become responsible for them all. I would never be able to walk past another again, and then I would have no time for anything else. It was easier to try to imagine that I had a right to ignore them and let them die but instead I bought fruit and brought it to her, determined not to be completely heartless. She was still groaning. I could see that she was emaciated with an awful ugliness of skin drawn taut around her skull. I wondered how long she had to live. I tried to give her some bananas. I peeled and broke one and raised it to her mouth, but her lips and tongue were dry and she couldn't bite or swallow. Two schoolboys joined me and bent over her. A woman walking past stopped to watch. So there were enough people willing to help if someone took an initiative. The dying woman spoke in mumbled Hindi but I could not understand her. The boys translated the weak sounds into more explicit Hindi, but I could not understand them either. I felt helpless. Swamiji would be wondering where I was.

I left the fruit and some money by her side and I walked away, leaving her, perhaps to die of thirst for want of a little more courage on my part. I had allowed myself to be directed by others every day I had been in India, and now I couldn't act on my own even to help a dying woman. I felt like trash. Five years later, I woke up in my bed in a flat in Belfast to see her face in front of me and to hear those groans begging me to do something in a language I still didn't understand.

Through the rest of my stay in India, when I came across starving people I tried to help a little. I fetched food and water for them and I notified the police. On one occasion I found a man who had crawled under the railway bridge at Jamuna Bazaar to die. He had no clothes on. He was filthy. There was a dry turd half in and half out of him and he hadn't the strength to shift it. He was groaning. I brought him food and water from a nearby stall and went to see a policeman whom I had seen earlier nearby. The policeman was a tall Punjabi Sikh. I said: 'There is a man under the bridge at Jamuna Bazaar and he is dying.'

'What you say. He is dead?'

'No, he is dying. Tomorrow he will be dead.'

'Well, tomorrow then we will take him.'

The saints I had read about as a child had been champions of self-sacrifice and charity. Father Damian kissed the wounds of the lepers on Molokai. The Catholic theology taught that it was good works, particularly towards the poor, that earned the grace which got you into Heaven. An Irish priest could never have walked past the starving woman at Kashmiri Gate and still passed himself off, at least to himself, as a saintly person. He might be a hypocrite who would not actually care and would only make a show of caring while others watched, but he would know even then that he was compromising a theology that forbade him to ignore her. Swamiji had no theological problem ignoring her. His responsibility was only to understand that the world was an illusion and not to get caught up in it.

He believed he was caught in the trap of karma like everyone else, living out the consequences of past lives, creating the conditions of future lives. Neither good works nor charity, nor anything that he devised by himself, would ever lead him out of it and free him from the need to be born of another mother. Only dispassionate rejection of everything would get him that. Fr Damian, seeking grace through actions, living among lepers and sucking their wounds, would, in Swamiji's view, only bind himself to a future life trapped by the actions of his past, condemned to perhaps indulge the comfort he had sacrificed or to wallow deeper in squalor, if that was really his heart's desire. Only indifference to his own suffering and to the suffering of others too, could have released him, according to the law of karma, as Swamiji understood it. And no wilful act initiated by a thinking self, however generous, could save a soul.

That was all very well, but I knew that I had finally allowed that woman to starve because I was unable to make the sacrifices that would save her. I had put my life above hers, and though that is perhaps what any sane person would do, it was anything but the grace of holy indifference that had enabled me to do it. Swamiji had made a deal with God, which was in a way the opposite of

Faust's deal with the Devil. Faust wanted to indulge himself and enjoy the best that the world could offer, and paid with his soul, Swamiji wanted his soul and was prepared to pay the world for it. He turned away from the world, that he might be wholly absorbed in God, or at least he affected to have done so and commended that course to me. What does it profit you to gain the whole world and lose your soul? That's the counter argument to Faust. But what does it profit your soul, to shun the whole world?

It had not been easy for me to go to India and settle there, but after some months with Swamiji I began to fret less about home and Linda and to enjoy the environment of Brig Ghat and the Delhi ashram. The ashram was next door to a *goshala*, a shelter for cows. In India, where the cow is sacred, voluntary Hindu organisations had been set up to care for strays. The ashram started out, I believe, as a *goshala* and then split from it. What happens is that those who find they can no longer afford to support a cow send it on its way with a garland of flowers round its neck, a devout prostration before it and a whack on the arse with a big stick. Swamiji's friends took in such cows and fed them.

Some were ill or crippled. One big grey animal had half a rear leg missing and spent its whole life trying to find the yard with a hoof that wasn't there. It repeated the same movement constantly of easing down its rear, expecting to find support. It seemed to discover each time anew that there was no support there and never came to accept that the leg it sensed there didn't exist. There was also a huge low-shouldered black English bull, donated to the *goshala* to lift the breeding stock, a project of which Swamiji disapproved – his commitment to racial purity extended to cattle.

It was the Mooneem family in the *goshala* who cooked meals for us. The lightest moments of my time there were when young Savita came with little treats of creamed rice or halvah.

We were working regularly on the *Bhagavad Gita* commentary and discussing it, and I began to think less cynically about some of the ideas Swamiji was trying to impart to me. Even without knowing anything about meditation, or much about altered consciousness, apart from smoking cannabis and twice taking LSD before coming to India, I could see that the external world was, at least partly, a mirror of the emotions, that it was more beautiful when the mind was not hungering for anything. At first the dry soil of India had scared me, as if the earth was as impoverished as the people who worked it. When I stopped worrying about this not being a place I knew, it started to feel like a place that knew me. I was still suspicious of Swamiji himself, and his prompting me towards meditation. I resisted, even though I was curious, because I did not want to commit myself further to him and, of course, reserve and scepticism were my legacy from life. Hadn't I had enough of dominant men trying to shape me?

Swamiji suggested that it was just a question of whether or not I could make a reasoned assent to an experiment in subservience and devotion. He was not being honest in this. This wasn't just an intellectual matter. I carried my scepticism around with me as a fixed quantity like the volume of blood in my veins. I had acquired it with some discomfort. It was my defence and I could not just unload it. Without it, I might be lacerated.

In chapter four of the *Gita*, Krishna tells Arjuna to acquire knowledge through prostration, enquiry and service. The implication is that it is only by service of a teacher that spiritual knowledge can be learned. At another point the *Gita* lists the characteristics of a wise person as humility, sincerity, harmlessness, forbearance, rectitude and, among others, service to the guru. In the *Katha Upanishad* we read: 'Wonderful is he who can teach about Him and wise is he who can be taught. Wonderful is he who knows Him when taught. He cannot be taught by one who has not reached Him and He cannot be reached by much thinking. The way to Him is through a teacher who has seen Him.'

No one was more revered than the guru. He replaced all other authorities. He alone was to be obeyed. Whatever the disciple was doing when the guru called, he stopped doing it and answered the call. In the *Devi Bhagwad Purana*, one of the scriptures of the Hindus, there is a line which says: 'If Shiva is angry, the guru can save; if the guru is angry, even Shiva cannot save.'

He who disrespects his guru is reborn a thousand times as a tree in a cremation ground, on which vultures gather. That's what the lore said. That is what Swamiji believed. What he was inviting me into was unreserved service to himself. The justification for a rigid guru-disciple system is that the goal of yoga is inconceivable to the mind that has not reached it. A mind that is not enlightened is said to be wholly unable to imagine the enlightened state or find its way to it. Only a teacher can take you there. One who is lost, says the *Chandogya Upanishad*, finds his way home by taking directions from those who know where his home is. Swamiji's assertion that he was qualified to be a guru carried with it the implication that he had seen the whole truth, that he had arrived at the state of *samadhi* and come to know that which is personified as God in all cultures and that he was in a position to guide me there also. I was never sure that this could be true. I was tempted. Indeed, at times I was fascinated by the idea of discipleship, of a relationship with an older, wiser man. Or was I just attracted back to a type of domination that was familiar to me from my childhood, by a karmic law that attracts the soul back to what it is familiar with until it is sick of it.

Swamiji sent for me one morning. He was sitting in the sun in a cane chair. I sat at his feet. He said: 'Now I will initiate you in the practice of meditation.'

He gave me a mantra, a one-syllable word, and asked me to repeat it to him. He looked tired. He told me to meditate by repeating the mantra in silence, keeping my mind fixed constantly on it, and he added another instruction: that I should imagine concentric waves spreading out from a point. Then he sent me to my room to start.

The mantra he gave me was a good word for conveying attentive feeling. It became both the object and the vehicle of concentration. I had thought that from then on I would be receiving almost daily instruction, but Swamiji held the same reserve from me as before and he discouraged questions. I returned to him the day after my initiation and he seemed perturbed by my effrontery and asked me to wait for an hour and return to him. It seemed that he could not deal with me unless he had time to prepare himself. He called me when he was ready and I went up and found him sitting in his deep cane chair. I bowed in the manner of a customary greeting and sat down.

'Yes, what is your question?'

I told him that in imagining concentric waves, these had become palpable around my head. The mantra seemed to get easily caught in the nerves like an automatic inner vibration. With an effort of concentration these waves could be coaxed to expand outwards on a horizontal plane, but when concentration was eas-ed, they tightened like a band around my skull. He said: 'I am glad to see that everything is developing as it should. Now, you should feel that this energy around you is benign and that there is no need for you to be disturbed or ill at ease. If you adopt an attitude of trust towards it, this discomforting phase will pass.'

He might have been speaking about our own relationship.

There was one other striking experience in the first days of my practice of meditation. I was sitting in my room, trying to keep my mind on the mantra, nervous and self-conscious in the dark. Then, in an instant this feeling intensified sharply, as if the dark-ness behind my eyes had come closer and I was somehow more present there, in a leap. I don't know if this scared me or if it was just the sensation of fear itself. Still, I took it for progress.

A few days later Swamiji invited me to go for a walk with him. He wanted to go to a nearby village to collect some reed mats for the ashram, and he wanted to meet the dealer personally, to nego-tiate a price. It was a bright, sunny afternoon. We walked together quietly, both of us relaxed and cheerful, now clear of the town and the highway. He had put off some of his authoritarian air. We over-took a villager walking home from the town and Swamiji asked him to go ahead of us to tell the mat maker that we would like to see him and that we would be sitting here by the path waiting for him.

'You will make very rapid progress in your meditation if you will have faith both in your technique and in your guru. You are a young man who wants to question everything. In a way that is good. But you know, this tradition is thousands of years old. It has been tested in successive generations. You can trust it,' he said.

This was the start of three years of deep, obsessive meditation. During much of that period I was so vulnerable that, had I been transferred in a moment to a European city, I would not have been able to function. I was turned deeply inwards and I developed my own vocabulary for describing things. No one, not even Swamiji, shared the experiences that I wrote about in my diary then. With no response from any other person, and confident that I was fol-lowing a path that others had taken before, and that it led to en-lightenment or the Beatific Vision, I pushed into the darkness that envelops the mind when the eyes are closed. I still wonder what was real and what was self-deception. Without a guide, I was open to every suggestion. When you find yourself sitting alone in your room, dwelling on your mantra in a most heartfelt way, and suffused with such joy that tears stream from your eyes, you know that a real happiness has overtaken you, even though you may not know what it is that you are happy about. It is as if you are in love and do not need to know who you are in love with. Was I in love with God or with Swamiji or with myself, or was I just feeling the great relief of past burdens falling away?

Swamiji wanted the love for himself. He wanted me to be wholly devoted to him.

He made a clear distinction between psychological growth and spiritual growth, but I couldn't and still can't. In the early months of my meditating for an hour or two, twice a day, holding my attention on the mantra, I found my mind perpetually wandering. My instruction was to disregard distractions and concentrate intently on the mantra, but this free wandering of the mind was therapeutic. Maybe it was, paradoxically, at least in the beginning, the most fruitful part of meditation. I began to remember things I had not thought of for years. It was as if, left to itself, while the conscious part of my mind tried to hold onto the mantra, the reflexive part went sifting through my whole memory, reliving and reassessing my past. I would be sitting on a folded sleeping bag on the bed in my room in the *dharamshala*, or at the Delhi ashram when we stayed there, reciting my little word, until once more it became a hum in my nerves, and vivid recollections of childhood would overtake me.

When I caught my mind wandering through memories, I would always realise that it had been doing this already for several minutes. This made me feel a failure as a meditator. The object was to stop thinking, but these inadvertent reveries took me through my past and reacquainted me with it. Sometimes memory would overwhelm me, with shame; the recollection of crass and stupid words, perhaps. Many of the memories seemed light and intriguing. I am sitting on my father's knee playing horsy. Or I am at the window of the living-room in Ballycastle, looking at the tiny irregular slabs of rainwater on the pane and wondering if it is true that a bogeyman lives out there beneath the dark shadow of Knocklayde.

Most of these memories came up to remind me that they were unresolved or did not fit neatly with my own account of my life. Without any willed effort, indeed while all the time trying to take my mind off myself, I would revisit past mistakes and humiliate myself. I was taking away my guard. The part of the mind that normally protected me from shame and guilt was engaged in the mantra, and these memories then sneaked into consciousness, often to appal me.

Anyone looking through the window at me might see me sitting with my legs folded, eyes closed, one moment calm and intent, the other startled, weeping or laughing. This was not the sort of examination of conscience that had been prescribed for us as children before confession. That was an active search for memories of sin, against a checklist of commandments. This was merely sitting exposed to the return of self-accusation. The sin might not have been a sin in any sense that the clergy taught. I recalled a missed opportunity with a girl I had met in a pub after work. It was obvious that she liked me. She drove me home and we talked alone in the car, but I didn't ask her to meet me again. My life might have taken a very different course if I had. The self-accuser said: 'You were daft! How could you not have seen at the time that that was an opportunity?'

Other moments like that came back to me, potential turning points in life that I had skirted for no good reason, out of nothing but inertia.

At times the past came back like a recalled flavour. There was a resonance or nerve-taste with the recollection of my awkward teenage years, a memory of how I had managed one long break from school prolonging an illness.

When I stayed home, I saw the streets empty of children and men and the estates given over to women. I saw the house as my mother had excavated it of furniture on the days when she cleaned, and followed her around watching her heft furniture and slop a mop or carouse with a little old vacuum cleaner that spewed as much dust from behind as it sucked in. She turned the kitchen into a factory and dripped hair and sweat over the huge washing machine and spin dryer that she wheeled out to the middle of the floor. After the clothes were washed in the drum, she hand-hauled them, and the water in them, into the separate spin dryer. A boy who fancied he was a man could be humbled by the sight of his mother exerting herself beyond his own ability.

An image came back from an earlier time. My mother grasps my shod foot into her lap, wedging the heel between her thighs, right against her stomach to tie my lace and says, 'Hold still, for God's sake'.

This sifting of memory and the humbling effect were probably worth more to me than the practised intentness of meditation and could not have been possible, as a deliberate, conscious probing of the past.

I began to feel deliciously vulnerable. I felt as if I was more centred in my breast, or as if my breast was a light membrane, and the concentric waves I dwelt on were perpetually generated from there. There is enough in poetry and song about the heart as the source of love for this to be familiar, yet in the most literal way, it seemed to me that, in that location in my body, I was warmed and tremulous.

Meditation, as I practised it, separated my emotions from their causes. I came to notice more the tangible manifestation of an emotion while discarding its content. If I was aglow in my breast with joy, I only assumed that this was because my spiritual energies were flowing well. It did not even occur to me to think that I was glad for a reason, let alone to ask what that reason might be. I was glad because I had a new structure in my life, and I had a new parent to look after me, because I had left behind the aimlessness of my three years in England which had seemed at the time the only escape from civil war in Belfast. I could relax and enjoy myself and feel little or no need to prove myself, and the very fact that I felt so happy, was evidence, to me, that I was in the right place, doing the right thing, according to destiny and God's will, and growing in spirit.

One of the problems you encounter when you fail to attribute your happiness to your circumstances is that you make ill-informed decisions on how to sustain it. A great idea occurs to you, an insight into where you are going, and you experience only the rush of enthusiasm; you don't heed the content of the idea, or even perhaps see what it is, because you do not recognise an idea as an idea, but think it is a moment of grace. You take time off work to walk along the river, and you do not reason that you are happy now because you have nothing to do. Instead, you imagine that some divine beneficence has settled on you, and you take this as proof that you are doing well in your meditation and becoming a holier person.

On one occasion, that ever-present sense of waves of energy became almost overwhelming. I had been anguishing over how to answer Linda's letters. She wanted to know if I was coming back to her. I didn't know. I was still in love with her and could not let go of my hopes of returning to her. That would become possible if I committed myself fully to Swamiji but I had not done that yet. I wanted the security of knowing that I could return to her, but I did not want to leave, and I knew that the longer I stayed the less likely she was to wait for me. I tried to meditate to still my own fretting, and after about an hour, when I opened my eyes, all my stress and worry suddenly recoiled on me. I had chosen Swamiji, or come to realise that I had already chosen Swamiji. I simply felt, however, that an intervention in my own personal space had taken the problem away. What was I to make of this moment of astonishment but that it was a solution, that it was grace, that it was from him?

Meditation did not always settle in the heart in this way, but it seemed sometimes to be entirely in the head. For instance, I would find myself just staring deeper and deeper into the darkness as if with an eye between my real ones. I became tense and restless, and I would find that when I lay down to rest or sleep afterwards, this tension would return and take over.

Swamiji moved to make use of my deepening commitment. He gave me a book on hatha yoga and prescribed a sequence of ten *asanas* – postures – for me to perform before meditation each morning and evening. He also asked me to get a picture of the goddess Saraswati and to visualise her when in meditation. Although I had been trying to keep my meditation non-religious, I accepted this idea. I went round the little shops in Chandni Chowk, a busy market street near the Red Fort, looking for an image of the goddess that I could be content to live with. The depictions of Indian divinities were mostly crass and gaudy, like figures from a comic book, though perhaps the image on our kitchen wall at home of the Sacred Heart of Jesus would have been as trite to an Indian eye. Our holy pictures were dark and solemn; the Indian ones were full of colour. Saraswati, the goddess whose image I was to visualise and meditate on, is the muse. Students worship her for exam success. She is the goddess of speech and writing. She rides a swan, which is the symbol of discernment, because the swan, in Indian mythology, can separate milk from water. She has four arms. Two play the *bina*, an instrument similar to a sitar, and in her other hands she holds a text and a *mala*, or rosary; these signifying, I think, that study and prayer are the same thing.

It is common to see Saraswati's statue in study halls, carved from white marble. I would have bought one of those if I had known where to look and had had enough money. Little sandalwood carvings of her are common too, but I did not like these because there was so little detail in the face. Some of the pictures were erotic; a lithe and thinly veiled body caressed the *bina* as if it was a phallic object of worship. I knew that if I meditated on that, I would get an erection during meditation. In the end I went for warmth and security, a crowned woman in a green sari, more like a solitary introspective woman than the potent urge behind all creative thought. I wanted her to be, as much as possible, a blank canvas on to which I might allow any feelings from within me to project themselves. I also wanted to be safe with Saraswati and not have her take a form, before my free imagination, that might scare me.

Most Indian icons present a raised palm to the worshipper, and I have read that this is so that when the image comes into view for the meditator, the first expression seen will be a reassuring one, 'Fear not'. I wonder if anyone who worships at an icon really believes that the representation before them is the creator of the entire universe. Surely even the apostles who followed Jesus Christ and sat with him by Galilee and listened to him talk about His Father, occasionally looked up at the night sky and felt not only that they were small, but that he was small too.

But love of an icon is a love that need not bewilder if it focuses the mind in an uncluttered coherence and directs all feeling at an image of someone who does not entangle you. The point is to be simple and direct, not to dwell on contradictions or images loaded with unsettling meaning. The Christian icons I knew from home were all of this bland character, showing expressions devoid of passion. Some of the Indian icons expressed rage or orgasm. The goddess might sit astride her man's loins, her hair thrown back and blown out like fire. The starry sky or the distant hills or the music of Bach may be unsettling when they awaken a nostalgia for something indefinable, but the statue of a reassuring god keeps things simple.

I surrendered to meditation. I found in it a space in which I could remove my guard against the world and other people, like some encrustation from my heart, some mask from my face. It was like going back to being the baby that I am and refreshing myself there. I discovered that that is what the mind wants to do; it wants to be vulnerable and enraptured. There are moments in ordinary life too when the intensity of the mind's engagement, whether in music or internally on itself, becomes rapturous. In that state, the mind sometimes feels content with its own existence and nature, and sometimes it hungers, but hungers delightfully, for a more refined condition.

There are moods of contentment that arise from sensory engagement with things which the body wants and enjoys, but there are also moods that arise when the mind feeds itself, when ideas or impressions build on themselves, when an accumulation of impressions seems to expand under its own momentum. These moods intimate the autonomy of the passive mind. Now this sufficiency may be an illusion. In a literal sense it certainly is an illusion, for if the body wilts and hungers then the mind suffers and no amount of reflection or music will lift it. Yet there are moments of contentment in which the assurance that all is well and all is always well is unquestionable and in which a benign glow from within, freed from all cynicism, is astonished and assured of love.

I can describe an occasion when this happened outside meditation, years after I left India. I was driving one rainy day up the steep ascent of the Glenshane Pass, on the road from Belfast to Derry. As I breasted the hill, several little things happened at the same time. The strain of the engine relaxed, and I relaxed too. The storm passed over and I emerged onto this new mountain landscape in which the dark underside of the clouds seemed to trap the golden sunlight and sharpen everything. Then the music on the radio became familiar; and it was the uplifting moment in an aria by Puccini, *O Mio Babbino Caro*. I knew it then only from the soundtrack of the film *Room with a View*. It was that gathering up moment in a song when you cannot help but sing along with it in your heart. The cumulative effect was such joy that I might have been flying.

That happened many times in meditation, in a dark room in India, to a man from Belfast, while cars honked on the main road, mosquitoes hummed close to his neck, and chanting from the Hanuman temple mixed with the sounds of cinema trails being blasted from speakers on lamp-posts. If this were a pathological state it would erode the spirit or turn the mind towards wasteful use of energy, but it always enriches life and affirms the sense of purpose. It is either nature's way of deluding us into plodding on, or it is a valid intimation of universal value. It brings us back to the original question: if we are merely tricked by nature, then life is not actually worth living, once we have seen through that; or this intimation is valid, and nothing actually matters that does not matter in that state of mind.

Perhaps these interventions are really from depths of emotion we had not known in our previous restricted experience and the mistake is to accept them as the final word of God and build our whole theology around them. I can believe now that the occasions of rapture and enthusiasm which I felt in India were natural products of travel and the shifting of context. They certainly seem more like the experiences described by travellers than the religious experiences recounted by people who stay at home.

I pass a simple farmhouse in the mountains on holiday and I suddenly know the person I would have been had I lived there and grown beans and read good books. This is not like a passion to own things. I don't look at a big car and feel that. The almost sensuous lust for a new computer or mobile phone can be silly and strong, but is not the same thing. I know that the house on the hill will never be mine. I know that I took paths away from that prospect long ago, but the person who might have been me living there is my ghost shadow now, fading from neglect, and I grieve for him.

Ted Simon describes several moments of extraordinary feeling in his book, *Jupiter's Travels*, written about his trip round the world on a motorbike in the 1970s. Every rough traveller must know the stretching of emotion and perception that comes with fatigue, uncertainty and discovery. Simon wrote, for example: 'As I think about it [the distance travelled], I have a sudden and extraordinary flash, something I have never had before and am never able to recapture again. I see the whole of Africa in one single vision, as though illuminated by lightning.'

He did not believe he had been given a vision as one of the elect of God; he was simply able to accept that as part of normal human experience, one may see and feel very deeply.

Strangely, Swamiji and his closest followers, seemed not to be concerned with achieving numinous moments but with fulfilling the forms of prescribed devotional practice. I was excluded from much of that because I was not a Hindu, but I doubted that there was much assurance available to me there anyway.

He was manipulative, and I had to be on my guard against that in him. I had known from the start that he would try to manage me to his advantage. His ponderous and daunting demeanour kept people at a distance. Sometimes, just by his acting as if something was natural or intended, he could make it happen, so long as others backed off and allowed it. He would give an instruction a lot more lightly than he would allow anyone to query it.

'Tomorrow we shall go to Delhi. I think it will not be too difficult for you to pack up everything and vacate your room.'

It would not have mattered to him how difficult that might be, or what plans I might have for the next day.

He often dictated his letters to me, for Walter Hartmann, his disciple in Germany, and I learned to help him construct the diplomatic phrasings which would hem Walter into doing something. Walter felt cut off from Swamiji. He had expected strong spiritual experiences of his own, and he was afraid that he would lose out on this by giving his time to teaching others. Swamiji wanted him to expand the teaching and to recruit disciples and donors for him. His letters to Swamiji were effusive and reverential, and the replies which Swamiji wrote patronised him and conceded nothing to his fears, but assured him that he was doing God's work and making sacrifices that would inevitably be rewarded with spiritual experience. In time, Swamiji even left it to me to compose some of these letters alone, and merely signed them. By then I had assimilated his devices. He was teaching me to substitute for him. I was willing to be used and controlled by Swamiji. I consented to being deceived, and I watched others do the same. I can hardly believe this myself or explain it when I think back on it. Did he hypnotise me or did I do that myself?

Hartmann joined us during the *Chaturmasa* in Bihar that summer. This was the two-month period of the monsoon, though the word *chaturmasa* itself means 'four months'. For this period, Swamiji was sworn to stay in one place and not to cross a river. It was the equivalent of Lent for him, a time of fasting and extra prayer.

Disciples often asked him to pass *Chaturmasa* with them and regarded it as a blessing on the household if he accepted. The monsoon, that year, produced little rain on the plains, though the air was thick and humid. Swamiji stayed with the Sharaf family in Deoghar, a small town near Jasidih, some stops beyond Patna on the Delhi-Howra line. The Sharafs lived in a large white house in a dismally poor village. The train journey from Delhi took thirty hours across the plains of the north at the hottest time of year, when much of the land seemed reduced to dust and it was hardly imaginable that the paddy would transform it into lush verdure within weeks. The Sharafs were a devout Hindu family who thanked God every day for their wealth and spent some of it on hospitality for holy men. They were feudal lords in the area. From a cane chair on his veranda in the cool evenings, Sharaf senior would hear disputes between his workers who fell on their knees before him and whined like frightened children. 'They are my subjects,' he explained to me.

Everything was harsher in Bihar. The mosquitoes were blacker and bigger. The poor were poorer. Beetles the size of walnuts staggered limply up to the overhang of the veranda, stunned themselves and rained like bits of broken biscuit upon us. Here Swamiji would be treated as royalty. No one would eat until he had eaten. I was low in the dining order and sometimes Swamiji would be finished his dinner and calling me out to work with him on the *Gita* commentary, before my own had arrived.

'Yes, you may go and eat it,' he would say, as if there was something generous in the permission.

As an untouchable, I was not allowed to enter the kitchen or handle any of the kitchen materials. I was allocated my own plates, cups and cutlery, and the servants were instructed in how to place the food on my plate, and take care not to make contact with it. Some of them dissented from the reverential management of Swamiji's demands. I saw enough cynicism in one man's eye to feel comfortable suggesting that he relax and let me take over.

He was a thin greying man of at least sixty, and I think he held these caste rules in contempt, for he grinned as I broke them, took my own chapattis by hand off his tray and lifted the little brass cruet to pour dahl onto my own plate. One day I walked into the kitchen and Abhay, the son of the family winced to contain his horror at the sight of me there. He knew that the whole room would now have to be washed; walls, floor and all, and that none of the food there would be eaten. I had gone to ask for water. I had asked a servant for it hours before and it had not come.

'There is no need for you to be here,' said Abhay. 'You should call a servant if you need anything.' He wanted to make it sound as if I was honoured in not being required ever to enter the kitchen. He was giving me permission not to go into the kitchen much as Swamiji had given me permission to have my dinner. The last thing he would have considered doing was explain to me that I was regarded as a contamination. I learned these rules from Walter Hartmann, when he came to us in Bihar. Hartmann was a candid and childlike man. He appeared to have complete belief in Swamiji, and his enthusiasm tended to dispel my own doubts.

'We are at the font of ancient knowledge', he told me with great enthusiasm, as we sat out on the veranda together in the evening. 'Ancient knowledge', he repeated, as if just thinking it amazed him. He would say: 'Swamiji has rules which we can never understand, but he understands them with spiritual insight. Spiritual insight. Ancient knowledge.'

Hartmann was vulnerable. He had marched with the German army in the 1940s and been weakened by that. When he was finally arrested, an American soldier struck him in the spine with the butt of his rifle, and he still needed support. He also suffered a detached retina, and had to avoid sudden jolts that might blur his vision. He moved gently, and he warmly patronised everyone around him. Later he would be disillusioned and appalled at how much money and effort he had poured into supporting Swamiji. I would meet him in Germany and he would try to trick me into eating a meat dish to wean me off my Indian vegetarianism, to save me from the last impress on me of the guru he had sent me to, but that summer in Bihar he would have kissed the feet of Swamiji, had he been allowed to.

Swamiji's obsession with controlling people and persuading

them that he was a spiritual giant became especially dangerous that year when he miscalculated his management of us, and employed devices which were crude and transparent. His skill had been in suggesting things, so that others might infer what he meant or intended. He would allow you to believe that a little coincidence was an example of telepathy, but he would not make overt claims about himself that he couldn't defend. Then he got blatant, and it was almost as disappointing as a lapse of style as it was unnerving to be under pressure. I did not want him to make it impossible for me to believe in him.

Hartmann had been pleading for a demonstration of spiritual power – that is, of magic – to prove that Swamiji had removed himself from the material world and gained power over it. Swamiji would be like Jesus, for Hartmann, if like Jesus he could work miracles. This was the last thing that I wanted. If yoga is about negation of the individual self, then it is not about power or control or about performance. If the only meaningful prayer is 'Thy will be done', then there is nothing prayerful in asserting control either by material or magical means. I had an instinctive sense that magic and spiritual maturity were conflicting aspirations, and that is what spiritual texts like the *Yoga Sutras* of Patanjali say, but Hartmann needed a demonstration of the power Swamiji had allowed him to believe he had.

It was hardly surprising that he would want this, and it may be that my aversion to it was not so principled as I imagined. If I had been shown a definite miracle, I would have had to decide that Swamiji was either a true spiritual guide worthy of total allegiance or a mage of some kind who was too dangerous to stay with. I knew that many of those around Swamiji lived with a belief in the immanence of the spirit world and accepted that magic and divine grace were routine parts of their lives.

Ghosts, for instance, were a common part of their experience. Santa Kumar, one of the 'boys' who served Swamiji, confided to me that he frequently sat up at night to converse with his dead grandfather. Another, Satya Shankar, was attacked by a ghost as he sat talking to me one night in Brig Ghat. He was telling me that he was frightened because a ghost had come to him in his room the night before. It was a tall swami in ochre robes, come to make demands of him. White fluid flowed from the ghost swami's head.

He ordered Satya Shankar to cover the wound. As he was telling me this story, Satya Shankar fell over screaming. That was an electric moment for all of us. He said later that the swami came back and kicked him because he was telling me about him.

That night, trying to sleep in the room next to Satya Shankar, I heard him talking for hours, pleading with someone for a little peace.

If I had been amenable to believing that our own Swamiji was a magician or a telepath, he would have been content to let me. To this day I do not actually know for sure if he exercised psychic power over me. Maybe he did. My horror was that on the day he chose to impress Walter, the trickery was obvious. One evening we came back from a walk in the bazaar to find Swamiji sitting at a table on the veranda, waiting for us. We sat down opposite him. Swamiji had a small book in his hand. It was neatly bound in brown paper. He said: 'Walter, I want you to write down the greatest problem you are experiencing in Germany in the teaching of meditation.'

Swamiji handed Walter a piece of paper, to write on, and the book to lean on. Walter used his own pen, leaning on the book, and wrote down his problem. Then he expected Swamiji to take the piece of paper from him but, instead, Swamiji told him to keep it. I thought at the time that he was using one of his suggestive techniques to get Walter to dwell on the problem and become receptive to proposed solutions.

Swamiji carried himself then in a colder, more authoritarian way than I had seen him do before. Now I think he was transparently defensive, but if you cannot think why someone should be on guard against you, you have to work out some other explanation for their rigidity, or confess bewilderment in the face of it. I found his manner distasteful and preferred to keep out of his way. Although I understood that he dealt with Walter differently, I recognised that he was manipulating both of us. I was able to accept this, because I trusted that he knew me and knew what was good for me. I was more perturbed by his manipulation of Walter than I was by his manipulation of me, because I knew, in the back of my mind, that I had already set limits to how far I would let him influence me and I thought that Walter had not.

That evening, Walter came to me to show me a piece of paper. He said Swamiji had given it to him. On it was written the same words which Walter himself had written in front of us that morning. He showed them to me and even the handwriting on the two pieces of paper was similar. The stated problem was 'No teachers for co-operation'. Swamiji had written underneath: 'Cause: With your present manner, you do not appear to be a genuine man of God. Solution: More inspirational techniques.'

Walter believed that he had witnessed a clear demonstration of psychic power. Swamiji had told him, he said, that as he had written the words, the thought had crystallised in his heart and become visible to him. Walter was happy with this answer. It promised him what he had wanted all along: technique. Unfortunately, the miracle which Swamiji had shown him was one which I could have reproduced myself with the help of a covered book like the one he had given Walter to lean on, and a piece of carbon paper under that cover. I had thought it strange at the time that Swamiji had handed the book to Walter, since he was usually averse to handing anything directly to either of us.

That night Swamiji sent Walter to find me and bring me up to the roof. I had been in meditation in my room when he knocked on the door. Everyone in the house knew by now that it was my custom to ignore knocking when I was meditating. Then Walter called out: 'Malachi, are you there?'

Still I ignored him and tried to maintain my light trance.

'Swamiji wants to see you now.'

I said nothing.

'Ah,' said Walter. 'I will tell him you are meditating.' He went away and I continued with my sitting. A moment later he returned and said: 'Malachi, Swamiji wants to see you now.'

So I got up.

I wasn't in a receptive state of mind. My reservations about Swamiji had made me restless and anxious. I had been concentrating hard to calm my mind and I had not succeeded. I had stilled it with hard work, as if by putting a heavy weight over the impulse to act or fret. Swamiji would see that I was hardened against him. I was accustomed to opening myself up to him almost unreservedly; he would see that I was not doing that. I walked up the stairs with Walter, past the kitchen, which had been out of bounds, onto another staircase I hadn't seen before and onto the roof. Swamiji was sitting in a cane chair. It was a hot night and he wore his robe around his waist with his big dark chest bare. I walked across and sat on one of two chairs that were set facing him. Walter walked forward too, but instead of taking his seat, he sat on the concrete.

Swamiji said: 'Is there some meaning in this? One sits at my feet and one sits on a chair at my own level.'

He had a way of saying things like this and sounding at the same time as if his interest was purely academic, suggesting that if people chose to be offended, that was their business and nothing to do with him. I sat on where I was. He spoke, at first generally, about my reading, which he said he was not satisfied with, and addressing his words more to Walter than to me. I asked him what he meant. He said he knew I had been reading *The Dhammapada*, a book with many misleading errors in it. I assumed he was referring to the chapter on the *Brahmin* which defines a *Brahmin*, not by birth, but by character and spiritual maturity. I did not argue. He wanted to draw me into a quarrel, to demonstrate to Walter that I was not a privileged disciple. This was all for him, not for me. It felt dangerous. If I argued with Swamiji he would demolish me. I did not respond. We would talk about it later.

Swamiji was now talking about a book that I would write about him, and he told Walter that it would be a good book. He had suggested this to me before but not discussed the idea in any detail. He said: 'While he is with me, I will give him the power to write this book and to write it well.'

He said that my journalistic experience would help: 'Though I don't know just how much experience you actually have.'

Swamiji was crass and bitchy but I swallowed it all and said nothing in protest. I would at least show him that I had learned from him how to do that. This was like a fight; him testing me to see how much humiliation I would take; me taking it, for fear that an open row would lead to my leaving.

In the morning I spoke to Walter about it. I didn't tell him my fears about Swamiji's 'miracle', but I said that I had been disturbed by his manner. 'But he was lovely. What is wrong?'

'He was bullying me.'

'Aw, it is your imagination. When you are talking to a man who has realised the Self and who is detached, you superimpose your own impressions on to him, and different people who are with him see him in different ways at the same time.'

This was the nature of the contest between me and Swamiji: how far would he be able to persuade me to concede that he was a spiritual giant, and how far might I be able to get him to entrust his frail vain humanity to me? The complication was that I needed him. I had nowhere else to go. I was fascinated by meditation and I was eager to believe that it was my destiny to be in India with him. The fantasy was exhilarating; that this was what I had been born to do, to pick up where I had left off my spiritual quest when last I had died. However, I could not let the trick with the book pass without letting him know I had seen through it. I did not want to expose him, though and have him admit that he was a fraud. I wanted him to restore my faith in him, and I hoped that he could and that he would never play such games again, at least not with me.

Walter went home to Germany and we returned to the ashram in Delhi. The days grew cooler and I passed most of them reading in the garden alone. Swamiji wasn't giving me much work to do. I was content like this. I had learned to enjoy being alone in peaceful places. My life was centred on meditation and in the preparation of the mind for it through the exercise of calmness and restraint. One day as I sat reading, I found myself breaking off frequently to look about the garden at the birds and the trees. I was keeping a wary eye on the clothes-line to guard it against the monkeys from the riverbank who frequently came in. My mind would not settle on my reading and I asked myself why. Then I realised that I had made a decision. I could not locate in memory the moment at which I had made it, but I knew now that I would confront Swamiji about the trick he had played on Walter.

That same afternoon I sat again for meditation in my room. I frequently experienced points of pressure on my head when I was sitting like this, usually on the brow or between the eyes, and these sensations always accompanied a mild entrancement that held my attention, almost magnetically, on the abstract. These sensations not only came when I was meditating, but whenever I was trying to concentrate, and they often drew my mind away from the immediate concern and swamped my thinking. This was a nuisance, but a manageable, even a pleasant, nuisance. That afternoon I felt a new point at the top of my crown, at first slightly off centre and then exactly at the centre. It was a prickly sensation at first and it changed the feel of my meditation. I had no sense that I was looking through this point, as I had through the point between the eyes. I was passive in relation to it.

Later I saw Swamiji at the back of his little cottage. He was carrying in his chair and was about to close the lattice doors when I went across to him and told him about this new sensation.

'Do you feel it right now?'

I was about to say no when it came back.

Swamiji said he would speak to me in a few moments. He closed the door, went through the cottage and out the other door onto another veranda. I went over and sat with him. He asked me to describe the pressure to him. Did it wriggle or creep? Was it light or heavy? Was it a soothing or a troublesome sensation? These questions meant very little to me then for the sensation was faint. I could say that it did seem, if I thought about it, that the sensation wriggled a bit. It was light and it was not troublesome. When I turned my mind to it, I became deeply absorbed.

Swamiji then said: 'Now you must begin to take your meditation seriously.'

'Recent events have distracted me.'

At first he assumed that I was talking about a long drawn out toothache that had only just been fixed by a competent dentist. 'Walter showed me the piece of paper which you gave him, duplicating his handwriting. He believes you performed a miracle.'

Swamiji sat silent with his legs folded under him and his arms resting on his knees, leaning forward in a relaxed and attentive posture, his hands clasped. He began to tap his thumbs together in agitation, as he often did when he was thinking intently, or worried.

'Very well. What is wrong with that?' So he was going to bluff it out.

'If you wanted to demonstrate a miracle, you should have chosen one that could not have been easily repeated, even by an amateur conjurer.'

His expression grew much sterner. We had a problem and now he was thinking about storming his way through it.

I said: 'I could do what you did.' He angrily waved me aside.

'How could you? Very well, show me how you could do it.'

Mr Chauhan, who managed Swamiji's practical affairs came

in then to discuss ashram business. He touched Swamiji's feet and they spoke together in rapid Hindi. Swamiji gave him his full attention, but when he had gone he turned to me again, to talk, not about the problem between us, but about other more general things. We passed several minutes then in complete silence.

I loved this man. I had caught him out, but I wasn't ready to string him up or leave him. He knew that. He said: 'It is absolutely essential to your spiritual progress that you should have deep faith in your guru.'

I didn't say anything to that. I had risked enough for one day.

That evening I exercised alone outside my room, walking up and down there rather than out along the river with Swamiji, which was the usual practice. I had a shower and then, feeling fresh and light I sat on my bed to meditate. I felt the point at the top of my head extend and wriggle. It seemed to sink into the skull and link the spot on the brow to another point at the back of my head. It was a novel sensation, as if there was a worm inside my brain. I felt an ache between my shoulder blades and particularly at the back of my neck. My concentration was deep, but with no object but my own vibrant mental space. I had much to think about and absorb from the conversation, but I did not even consider that this sensation was stress or relief or anything at all to do with the emotions of the day.

I had wilfully initiated the process of meditation, but I was coming to a point where no effort was involved and a natural spontaneous flow of vibrant energy carried my mind with it. The vibration now seemed to be planing out, reducing my sense of the body so that I seemed weightless. I sat like that for about ninety minutes and I could have continued but I didn't want to be disturbed by Satya Shankar bringing my evening meal. After my meal, Swamiji called me. Usually he didn't call me at this time unless he had urgent work for me. He stood in the middle of the lawn and I approached him apprehensively. He said: 'What was your meditation like this evening?'

I said that it had been very deep and steady.

'How long did you meditate for?'

'For about ninety minutes, but I could have gone on longer.'

'Very well.' He said no more. He had made his point. He was taking the credit.

In the morning I rose early and took a walk along the promenade by the Jamuna. When I came back, I performed my yoga asanas in my room and sat again for meditation. This time I could not get into it. My mind wouldn't settle into steady concentration. Nothing happened: there was no vibrancy, no sense of an automatic wellspring of energy lifting me. I might as well have been browsing through a newspaper for all the depth I could find. I was exasperated and disappointed, though I tried to be stoical. Then Swamiji called me out again and asked: 'How was your meditation this morning?'

'It was dull. Nothing to talk about.'

'You must cultivate a deep and abiding love for your guru if you want to make progress.' The hint was that he was showing me a trick that I could not see through, and that until I was at his level I would need him.

'Well, let us let things rest. Let there be no conflict,' I said.

'You must have no reservation about your guru.' He wanted me to concede that he had won.

With difficulty I said: 'There are no reservations in my mind.'

I rationalised this to myself as meaning that I was not puzzled by what he had done, but I allowed him to believe that he had won me over. I was a coward. I knew this only deferred the problem. He must have known himself that co-operation that had been bullied out of me meant nothing.

After that morning there was no recurrence of the vapid meditation. The spot on the top of my head grew more and more palpable and it seemed, at times, almost as if the whole top of my crown was a drum skin being pressed down from above or out from within. By the beginning of November my sittings were deep and serene with very little pressure on the spots, but with a gentle outdrawing sensation from the top of the head and with light even breathing that created no distraction. I seemed to be losing all desire to express myself. Writing in my diary, I might stop in mid-sentence with no will to go on.

I read *The Imitation of Christ* by Thomas A. Kempis. I could not accept it as a guide to living, yet by reading it, I subdued my own wilfulness and chastened myself in such a way that when I sat on my bed in the evenings with my legs crossed, I felt as if I was going cap in hand before God. My sittings were getting longer.

Often I would sit for three hours at a time in this attitude of humility. The first hour might be dull as I worked to evade the distracting tatters of thought that blew about my mind, but joy would come slowly seeping through my breast and I would feel my head begin to expand. At times the spots at the brow and at the top of the head seemed parts of one internal organ. These sittings were so peaceful, I felt I might float away.

But I began to feel, during other times, a disturbing flicker across my brow and it hampered my concentration. One day Swamiji said that there was an expression of strain on my face and I told him that there was a storm going on in my brain, for that seemed to accurately describe the ripples which I felt around my head, emanating from the centres. He seemed anxious. He said: 'You should have told me earlier.'

There was a full moon that night. I sat on my bed facing the wall. It took me about an hour to find peace and then, though conscious, I was as relaxed as if in sleep. And I felt the top of my head pulsing. I was as fully concentrated as I could be and there was very little distraction in my mind. I began to feel my body drawn taut and erect and it seemed as if my head was being pushed back. My neck hurt because of the weight of my head. The small of my back ached. I felt occasional distensions of the top of the head, as if it was a membrane being inflated by sharp injections of air.

In the third hour of my sitting, this feeling grew more frequent and stronger. I can't imagine that it was an hallucination. Of course, it wasn't the solid bone that was expanding, but it felt as if it was. Then something palpable touched my shoulder and moved me into a more erect position. That's a detail that I would like to leave out so that everything else would be more plausible, but it happened. I felt as if I was in the presence of someone else and that someone was helping me through these strange events. I was like a child sitting in a mother's lap waiting to be shown some marvel.

The balloon that my head had become, expanded, and I became more engrossed, amazed almost, and the tension between the inner part of it – myself – and the outer part, arrived at an equilibrium in which I felt as light as air and more comfortable than I had ever felt before. This placid, enthralled, enlarged body was now more real to me than my physical body. Then, after a few moments of this comfort, my heart started beating wildly, my breathing accelerated and I felt a rapid flickering at my side, under the ribcage on the left. The pitch of my brain intensified as if power was rushing into it. The power had a definite electrical quality. It seemed that the electrical nerve impulses had been immensely amplified.

I felt myself rising out of my body. I was alone and afraid. My physical body was suddenly clamped rigid so quickly that the bones of my spine were forced into position with an audible crack. My body shook and quivered and the wall of the inflating balloon, extending in sudden pulses, seemed to go beyond all palpable awareness. The muscles of my face convulsed. I was breathing heavily and noisily and without control. I was slavering and my heart was beating so hard that I thought it would burst. I felt as if a murky rag was pulled away from my eyes and now the energy coursed through me like the rush of flame in a blow torch and I let go of all physical sensation, transformed into a ball of energy, floating, more clearheaded than I had been in my life before, as if my mind was now free from the awful clogging that a body is.

And this was normal. This was right.

I was still conscious of the room. I heard a mouse on the floor and after some minutes the rushing flow of electric power subsided and I gradually regained physical feeling. When this subsidence began I saw a very clear white image of my mother in her younger days, as I remembered having seen her in an old photograph, taken perhaps before I was born. The first part of my body that I became aware of was the top of my head. I moved from spot to spot, to the top of the brow, the centre of the brow and the point between my eyes and slowly recovered feeling in my trunk. The last part to come back to me was my legs and as soon as I felt them, I was shocked by the pain in them, fell back and screamed. This was awful. Were they broken? I managed to straighten them slowly and get the circulation flowing again, so that I could relax, take my mind off the pain and think about what had happened.

I was as exhilarated as the day when I jumped into the sea in the dark with a life jacket on, thought I was drowning as I plunged, and then bobbed to the air. This had been an adventure, like falling from a height, narrowly missing death. The astonishment, on reflection, was itself overwhelming, like the relief of unexpected survival.

I heard Swamiji talking outside my room and I was anxious to go to him and tell him what had happened. I staggered to the door. My legs were hardly strong enough yet to hold me. When I looked at his face, I saw it as being as white as snow, like the image I had seen in my mind of my mother. It was as if there was some residual white light in my head bleaching what I looked at. I tried to speak but I couldn't find words to express my feelings or to articulate what had happened. I didn't know what had happened. In some strange way it seemed as if it was not me to whom this had happened anyway, at least not the embodied and confused me who now stood before him. Or perhaps I sensed that it had nothing to do with him. Could anything be more personal than this sudden eruption? It was as if I was running to Brother Gibbons to tell him about my first orgasm. What would he have said but that I should pray?

My brain was buzzing. I shook my head and said nothing. Swamiji told me to go back into my room and relax. As I walked in, I saw a mirror on my bookshelf and I looked at my face. It was beaming with delight and energy like a happy child's. I wasn't stuck for words to express to the mirror. They were 'Wow! Fuck! Jesus!'

Swamiji sent food to me but I couldn't eat it. Then he called me out and asked me again what had happened. At first I could find no words. Then I remembered from the *Gita* commentary the phrase 'like a candle in a windless place'. This seemed to describe the steadiness of the energy flow, but Swamiji misunderstood me.

'You have seen the light?'

No, I had not seen light.

I didn't sleep much that night. On the following morning, when I sat for meditation, I was surprised to find that immediately I closed my eyes, I became conscious of a strong flow of energy through my body to my head. It wasn't nearly as strong as the actual eruption of the night before, but I felt that if I allowed it to grow, it would get that strong again. The energy intensified in my brain and I seemed to be surrounded by a taut aura. It felt as if every nerve in my brain was stretching and my skull was expanding. There was a sharp dilation of my sinuses too and they clicked open audibly. Again I was unsteady on my seat, rocking slightly, as if the earth itself was moving. The sequence I had gone through the night before was starting up again. I was also, now, more afraid. I rose without letting it go any further. I did not want to be overwhelmed.

Throughout the day I was restless and edgy, though I was often buoyant too. My resolve, cultivated under Swamiji's instructions, to curtail the spontaneous activity of my mind, the chatter and the singing and the daydreaming, had now been revoked. My mind had come alive and would not be curtailed. I was singing or chatting to myself all the time. Yet, at moments, I would also be overcome by a feeling of indifference to life and I would lie in my bed and feel that vibrant tingle in my brain again. It was as if my brain was overworked with thoughts and anxieties even when there was no conscious thought in my mind at all. I was thinking, but what was I thinking?

In that state, what thoughts did come to my mind often came with a clarity that jolted me. I recalled an act of vandalism from my teens and I was so rent with shame that I had to get up and walk around the room to shake off my horror of myself. In the evening, when I took my exercise, pacing up and down, I felt light on my feet; jubilant. When the boys in the ashram came to watch me or talk to me, I would strike a pose for them, perform a little mime, make them laugh.

When I sat for meditation, I felt that great build up of energy again, as if I was a bomb about to explode, and again I shied back. That night Swamiji called me. He was sitting on the veranda with Chauhanji on a mat at his feet. He sent for a chair for me and let me sit at his own level. I was not keen to talk frankly with Chauhanji there. Swamiji just said that I should observe mental changes in myself and write them down. 'An observation of your state of mind in the coming days will render clues as to how the world is to benefit by what has happened'.

I asked him if I had had an experience of *samadhi*, and he said that I had not. Evidence of this was that several normal functions had continued during the experience. He said that I was mistaken in my impression that I had left the body. 'When you leave the body, the body dies.'

The next day he told me he was going to Amritsar and that he would be away for about a week. I was frightened of being left behind without him at such a time and told him so, but immediately I felt ashamed of myself. It wasn't going to make any difference whether I was afraid or not. He was going and I was staying.

I had started work on the book he had asked me to write, and he wanted me to continue with it while he was away. He also advised me to restrict my meditation to one hour in each sitting. I felt this was a great limitation to have to observe, for though the sittings since the eruption had unnerved me, I still wanted to get back to stable and blissful meditation. He told me it would be wiser for me to concentrate on building myself up physically. He said: 'You should make yourself so strong that you can throw another man to the ground, though, of course, you must never actually do that.' And he laughed.

I was now entering a new honeymoon period with Swamiji and I felt able to put my faith in him again. The dramatic developments in meditation seemed to authenticate his guidance. He had said meditation would lead to profound insights into the nature of the soul, and that is what appeared to have come of it. I was vulnerable and I needed his strength on my side. He left for Amritsar, and I tried to set up a routine of working on the book, but I found that I couldn't concentrate on it without quickly getting restless. I went into the garden and tried to relax, but began to feel guilty about not working. Moving about, I would experience strange cut-out sensations in my mind. I would be walking across the garden and after a few steps, I would feel a sudden awareness of my situation, as if I had woken up just there. Then a few steps on the same experience would recur, as if my mind was surprising itself over and over again. I was still reeling, but I had nothing with which to interpret that experience, other than the teaching of Swamiji, that meditation unfolded the soul. That being the case, I should only continue to meditate and hope that this orgasm in my brain would happen again. What I realised from it at least, was that this is natural, that we are made for this to happen. It made me feel a bit like a punctured tennis ball with a dent that is usually only ever displaced, never removed. For some minutes I had been round again.

It had been a recoil, overthrowing my self-discipline, restoring spontaneous wit and energy, and yet at the same time, being such a dramatic result of meditation, seemed to confirm that I was right to continue with the discipline. I was frightened of meditation after that, however. When I began to feel energy rising in that way again, my own apprehension brought self-consciousness back in and that cut the process off. I was never able to wholly forget myself. The eruption I experienced was the shakedown I needed to restore my vitality, but it was years before I understood that. I was distracted by the conviction that it had been a spiritual event rather than a natural one. Now I am not sure there is a distinction to be made there.

I was elated. I had an enormous sense of grandeur at times, a sense of being privileged, a sense that I was a more evolved human being, closer to superconsciousness than those I passed every day in the street. Perhaps I was a prophet. This wasn't supposed to be the effect of yoga and meditation. They were supposed to restore my meekness and innocence. That should have been enough to make me doubt the course I was on, yet, when a wonderful woman turned up to distract me from all this, I resisted. I preferred to stay on my path to enlightenment.

Swamiji believed that it was always love, or what he called concupiscence, which threatened a holy man's commitment. St Kevin of Glendalough is said to have been pestered by a woman who loved him, even in his hermitage, and threw her down a hill to save himself from her temptation.

Walter Hartmann – whatever he had been thinking of – sent Gerlinde Obermeir, an Austrian playwright, to the ashram. He said that she had been having trouble with her meditation and had been hospitalised as schizophrenic. It never occurred to any of us that her madness was really anything but a difficulty in her meditation practice. I knew that I too could easily have been perceived as mentally ill if I had returned to the west when I was most absorbed.

Gerlinde came on the first day of the monsoon. Swamiji was out of town. The ashram garden was flooded and a pair of young monkeys splashed about in the muddy water. The cook called me out of my room. He was standing looking amazed at this blonde woman in jeans and a blue sweatshirt who had not understood that she should have taken off her shoes before walking on holy ground.

For four or five days I accompanied Gerlinde around Delhi. Mr Shanker, a lecturer at the university and an old friend of Swamiji's, gave her a room in his home, but she could not relax there. She did not eat and did not sleep and we presumed this was because it was so hot and humid. I could see that she was often edgy.

Perhaps I was unnerving her by suppressing my own interest in her. I tried to be strong and supportive and I tried to be wise and witty, but her uneasiness increased in the coming days and I only ever managed to assuage it for short periods.

She had an almost frantic expression at times as if she lived on the edge of calamity, but the same emotional rawness enabled her to slide into giddy and often raucous laughter. The expression she wore most often, however, was anxious confusion, and she often pleaded for help and reassurance.

We sat in the park in Jor Bagh one afternoon. We had gone to town initially because she wanted to buy presents for her daughters, but she had not been able to relax, so I had brought her here to calm her.

'Do you ever feel?' I said, 'that your own nervous energy is an aura of power active in your body and around it?'

'Yes,' she said. She was looking straight into my eyes and I was looking straight back into hers. She seemed to feel she could find security by staring at me. Were we supporting each other or maddening ourselves?

I would try to be light and dismissive and not to allow this kind of hypnotic libidinous tension to arise because I was not willing to fall in love. I didn't know that this ache in my breast was desire. I pretended there was no desire in me and yet I toyed with the ache and nurtured it and explored it as if it had no relation to the normal magic of a celibate man and a buoyant woman meeting and wanting to get hold of each other.

On the day that Swamiji came back from Amritsar, Gerlinde came to the ashram with the Shankers to meet him. Over her skirt and blouse Gerlinde wore a sari which Mrs Shanker had wound round her, though it was hot.

Swamiji was in his room and the three of them waited on the veranda. I crossed the garden to speak to them, though I felt that this was not my territory on that side of the lawn now that Swamiji was back.

'Did you sleep well?'

'No,' she said. 'I was afraid.'

'What were you afraid of?'

'I don't know. I was thinking about a man in Germany who practises telepathy and I was imagining that he could hurt me.'

I said she should talk to Swamiji about it. I didn't even consider that this was a fear of Swamiji breaking through in her dreams.

Swamiji came out and looked first at me. I expected him to be stern with me because of my familiarity with Gerlinde and this must have shown on my face.

He said: 'You look a little bit unwell.'

He sat down slowly, saying nothing yet to the others, withholding his attention, as usual, until he was in a position to give it completely. Satya Shankar spread out some straw mats on the floor and the four of us sat down, Mrs Shanker first prostrating herself according to custom at Swamiji's feet.

Chauhanji arrived then and he took his place among us too.

It didn't surprise me that Gerlinde was uneasy in Swamiji's presence. She didn't know how to behave. She certainly wasn't going to prostrate herself, but she wasn't sure that it wasn't expected of her.

Swamiji asked her directly how she felt.

She was slow to answer. She couldn't know whether this was a casual enquiry requiring only a superficial answer, or a serious request for full knowledge of her condition. She laughed nervously and glanced towards me for support. I didn't give her any.

'I am not sleeping well.'

'You must relax when you are here with me and not worry about anything. Your health will improve. Be sure of that.'

Then he turned to speak to Chauhanji in Hindi, for he had business with him. Gerlinde listened to this for a while, understanding nothing, and she looked edgily around her, but we all sat quietly in deference to Swamiji, and then she got so uneasy that she got up and ran across the lawn to my room. Swamiji signalled to me to go and see what was wrong. I found her sitting in tears. She had taken off the sari and she held it up with disgust, as if to blame it for all her discomfort. Then she said; 'It's hopeless. I don't know what to do. Does he think I am going to touch his feet?'

She was very angry.

I was alarmed. I was anxious too. I knew well enough how Indian society tended to direct people in their behaviour. It would only be normal if Gerlinde rebelled against all the pressures that I had yielded to. And that frightened me. It would leave me with greater doubts about my submission to Swamiji. I tried to soothe her. 'That is just the custom of the country. It is not expected of you.'

I knew well though that Swamiji wanted me to adopt the custom of bowing low before him, and would no doubt be content to have Gerlinde greet him as the other women who came to the ashram did. 'He sits there on that chair and you all sit at his feet as if he was some dignitary. I feel very strange. I do not know what to do or to say.'

When she'd spent her feelings on the matter she laughed. I was relieved and I brought her back to the group.

'What was the matter?' said Swamiji. I spoke up for her this time. 'The sari she was wearing was too hot for her and she was embarrassed to take it off because it was Mrs Shanker who put it on her.'

Gerlinde wiped her eyes with the heel of her hand and laughed. I smiled and she laughed louder, happy again and relaxing and trusting that it was all right to laugh, though Chauhanji and the Shankers were probably horrified. 'Excuse me, excuse me. I am sorry,' she said.

'But what for?' said Swamiji.

'For laughing.'

'Never apologise to anyone for laughing,' he said. I was enchanted by Gerlinde and her giddy elations, which I believed I recognised as the same joyful state that I had known through meditation. I did not know enough to be suspicious of elation then. When she told me that she was terrified that she might die, that she felt the top of her head lifting, I said this was all good and so just frightened her further.

One of the stresses was speaking English all the time. She was often trying to speak English to people who had addressed her in Hindi. Mrs Shanker chatted away to Gerlinde in Hindi, so I suggested that Gerlinde answer in German. What difference would it make? But it just confirmed to others that she was insane. I was the last to believe she was cracking up, but she was. I found her one morning wandering near Mr Shanker's house. She looked drawn but joyful, like someone with no more restraints. She said: 'I told Mr Shanker I do not love him. I told him I love Malachin.'

She had read my name as Malachin from Hartmann's handwriting and was amused to see the mistake when she met me, but now I was Malachin again. The next two days were the longest of my life. She asked me not to leave her and I said I wouldn't. She picked up a piece of paper and started to write. I took it from her. She had written in English: 'I will not leave Gerlinde.'

'What's this for?'

'I am writing down all your promises and then you can sign them.'

I walked her to the ashram and we arrived during Sunday morning *satsang*. When it was over I called Satya Shankar and I asked him to tell Swamiji that I wanted to speak to him. Shortly afterwards Swamiji came out onto the patio at the back of his cottage and called us to him. He looked severe. He said he would not normally speak to me at this time, that it was his custom to give his full attention to the people who came to his *satsang*.

'What is wrong?'

'She is in a vacillating emotional state. She seems at times to be deluded,' I said.

Swamiji turned to her. 'What is your problem, Gerlinde?'

She snapped angrily at him: 'I am not here to kiss your feet.'

'Has anyone asked you to kiss my feet?'

She turned on me. 'Why do you let him talk to you like that? Why do you not stand up to him?'

'There's no need to stand up to him. He's trying to help,' I said.

She grabbed my hand. 'Come. Let us go away from here. Let's leave him.'

I stared into her eyes and she stared back into mine.

'Now, sit down.' She obeyed me and sat down, as if I had hypnotised her.

'Obviously you are the one with some control over her, so you should stay with her,' said Swamiji.

Swamiji could do nothing for her. He only wanted me to keep her away from the ashram. We used the cheap hotels of Delhi, but didn't sleep. One night she took off her jumper and used it as a cushion for two little star badges she wanted to present to me. What she was actually presenting me with was her breasts, but I was determined to be celibate.

It was harder to keep that resolve when she recovered. I persuaded her to take sleeping pills and after she had found her balance she said she wanted to go to Kahmir. I offered a compromise. Rather than let her go into the mountains alone, I would take her to Nainital, which was not so far away.

We took the overnight bus to Nainital and the journey was long and tedious, though it was a relief to be together without having to answer to anyone but ourselves. I was still determined to be a true *sadhaka*, yet I knew what was going on, that there was freedom and romance in the air and that it was already overdue. So I was deceiving myself and confusing Gerlinde.

Most of the other passengers on the bus were poor Indians who had paid about a week's wages for their tickets. There was a young graduate who had been westernised by the Irish Christian Brothers. I wondered if the Brothers themselves saw any contradiction between what they had done to him and their job at home of turning young Irishmen into ardent republicans.

There were a couple of French boys on the bus dressed in rags, but they didn't speak to us, so I got no idea of what motivated them, but I guessed it was either drugs or religion or both. We stopped for tea and toilets near Brig Ghat and later in Moradabad, and the dawn was rising through the mountain mist when we reached the foothills.

Gerlinde lay slumped across my lap dozing. She can't have been comfortable. I wasn't. It might have been a soft pillow when she first went down on it but she was content and not at all embarrassed, and she made no comment when I moved her so that I could stretch and rearrange myself. Nainital was a tamed and manicured valley by a sumptuous ribbon lake, a holiday town with few signs of poverty save the anxiety of the luggage porters at the bus stop clamouring for custom. We walked to a wood-built hotel on the main street and took two large rooms on the top floor overlooking the lake, for ten rupees a night each. Then, because we were too excited to sleep, much as we needed to, we went out for a walk.

We didn't go far. The town reminded Gerlinde of Austria with its chalets, the forest covered hills and even its large steepled church. We were tired. Our spirits slumped and we wanted to get back. A man came and offered us a ride on his horses but we couldn't accept.

'Oh, I am so tired,' she said.

'Me too. I must go to bed. I think I could sleep the whole day.'

She said: 'I have a strange feeling on the top of my head, as if it is lighter than the rest of me and wants to float away.'

'How do you mean?'

'There. Just this spot at the centre.' She laughed. 'It is moving up and down.'

'Have you ever felt that before?'

'No,' she said.

'I think you must go to bed and sleep, and we'll meet again in the afternoon.'

She seduced me in Nainital and it wasn't difficult. One day she asked me to hold a towel round her while she changed into her bikini to swim in the lake. She dived into the water and emerged seconds later some yards away from the circle of ripples she had made. She was a powerful swimmer.

Two boats converged near her, full of young men coming to look. They whistled and called to her. She was not afraid of them, or even very annoyed, just exasperated that they had behaved so predictably.

I stood above on the bank and tossed stones close to the bows of the boats, in the hope that they would see that they were not welcome, but not under attack either. They cheered when Gerlinde stepped dripping from the water, and they could see her bottom through wet cotton. She dried and changed, while I held the towel round her again, and we went back to the hotel, close together under the umbrella, for it was raining now. We had lunch in a restaurant and then went to our separate rooms to snooze.

I was restless. I wanted her, and yet I wanted to be a disciplined *sadhaka* and resist her. After an hour I heard her rise and go out. She paused a moment at my door. I got up and called her back. She could lie beside me and talk, but we didn't talk.

Gerlinde must have felt she was with two men.

I treated her coldly and approached her mechanically, nervous, but hoping to be in control of my emotions, and ashamed of myself for breaking Swamiji's rule. I asked her to undress, but was slow to undress myself, deceiving myself that I could simply gratify my curiosity about her body. I saw the little stretch lines on the body of a woman who had had children. There was a life written on her body. In the end it was brief, a release of tension, with my emotions withheld so that I might retreat back into my ascetic convictions, with my nagging need for her put to rest for a while. It would have been kinder to masturbate, but equally a breach of the rule. In those days the only time I had orgasms was in my sleep.

I tried to recover my distance from her, then drew her back in again. I was trying not to let her get close, and trying also not to shove her away. I didn't want to be her lover but I wanted her to want me so there was always tension, but sometimes there was fun. We became clowns together. One day I said to her, 'Show me your tits and I'll give you a rupee.'

She laughed and pulled up her jumper. Later, in front of Swamiji, I turned to her and said: 'Here's that rupee I owe you,' and stared at her, daring her to keep a straight face.

It wasn't till her last night, when she was ready to fly back to Austria that we made love – without me feeling reservation or guilt – in my room in the ashram, with Satya Shankar audibly moving about outside. It was simple and amicable, not passionate, just a token thing as far as the sex itself was concerned. It was what we had both wanted from the day she arrived.

I spent a third Christmas by the Ganges, barely conscious of what day it was. Swamiji stayed in Delhi; I managed affairs at the ashram construction site. My chief companion was Satya Shankar. Occasionally, men like Satya Shankar came to stay with Swamiji, to work close to him, in the hopes of finding jobs in Delhi through contact with his followers, many of whom were business people. He and the other ashram servants lived stressful lives; they were poor and anxious, but serving an ashram, maintaining the garden, cooking the meals and playing music during *satsang* was an easier life for them than cycling a rickshaw, the only option for many others like them in the city.

I liked Satya Shankar, but we were separated by many things; chiefly his poverty and his cultural assumptions about the west. He had a sarcastic humour. Sometimes his lips parted at the side and bared his teeth in a mocking growl. He saw through people, yet sometimes he would revert to apologetic frankness, when he had to manage things for practical advantage. I was the same way with him, playful but setting limits. I was wary of his criticisms of Swamiji because I was determined to think well of him at this time. I was appalled sometimes by Satya Shankar's own simple religious conservatism. There was a girl who visited the Delhi ashram with her parents. She was plump inside the baggy frock shirt and trousers of the unmarried, and she often had her schoolbooks under her arm. I had asked Satya Shankar if he was looking for a wife. I teased him about this girl. 'But, Mr Malky, she does not have a good reputation.' I told him to fuck off and get some sense.

Together in Brig Ghat, Satya Shankar and I arranged the purchase of cement and the supervision of work on the construction site. This was the most pleasant time of the year; the sun shone every day. Two or three times a week I treated myself to a long walk along the bank of the Ganges, absorbing into myself that rarefied light of the glinting river, intimately cavorting with nature, indulging as I had never done before, nor have since, a feeling of closeness to a personal god in the natural world. This was a free and blithe time, a time of adventures with Ganga; Ganga, the river I bathed in, the river I swam in, the river I followed for a few miles in either direction from the town, the river whose breast I sailed on, the river whose water reflected the night sky to me, whose water on occasions I was foolish enough to drink. Ganga.

When I returned to Delhi in March I was ill, probably with hepatitis. A *brahmacharya* replaced me at the ashram building site when Swamiji asked me back. I did not know at first that I was ill. Dramatic disturbance in the stomach was frequent, at that time of year, but usually passed quickly. The ominous sign was an attack of colic which doubled me up, and which passed as suddenly as it came. I was also short of money. Walter had been sending money to me through an Indian bank every three months, but an instalment was late. And then Swamiji announced his plan.

I sat with him one evening, on a reed mat while he crouched in his big wooden chair. He asked me how I was and I told him I had been unwell. I said I was still lethargic and had little appetite. He told me to take more exercise to shrug off whatever malaise was still clinging about me. Swamiji adopted his most magisterial air and leaned over towards me with his big fleshy hands folded. This was a posture he adopted when he wanted to be persuasive.

'I have designed a garb for you, and if you wear it, I will send you to Germany to teach yoga there with Walter.'

'What sort of garb?' I did not have the confidence to reject the idea outright, so I worked through the details. I was excited by the idea of going to Germany and working with Walter, but I did not fancy walking through city streets dressed like a monk.

'A silk garb. A yellow silk garb, like that of a *brahmacharya*, but with blue bands at the cuff. You understand the idea of wearing a garb?'

I said I did. It set you apart, and that was supposed to secure a space for you in which your spiritual quest would not be disturbed. I had no argument against this, since I had already agreed to discipleship. If I rejected the idea of a garb, then I was admitting that I was not wholly committed to *sadhana*. Anything I would say against wearing a garb would smack of defending the ego that I was daily working through meditation to extinguish. I don't want to wear it; it's not my style – arguments like these had no weight.

'I am not a Hindu,' I said, 'and I am not here to adopt Hindu ways, but simply to help you with your writing and to learn meditation.'

He reacted with distaste, and said smugly: 'So you hate Hinduism.'

'No, I do not hate it, but so much of what is religion here seems trivial to me. I have no wish to identify myself with Hindu culture. I am impressed most strongly with what I think is the essence of Hinduism, which is the *Advaita Vedanta*.'

The *Advaita* is the philosophy of the one pervasive Self, suffusing the whole cosmos, the ultimate reality on which the whole universe is like a vapid stain. The yogi who could see clearly, at the end of the journey would see that there was nothing else but That, the Self which is known as Sat Chit Ananda, Being, Consciousness and Bliss, about which nothing else can be said. Swamiji said: 'The *Advaita* is the core of Hinduism. Indeed it is the whole of Hinduism, as you will see when we have discussed this further. Then, I am sure, you will come round to my way of thinking.'

We parted in good humour, but I was apprehensive for I knew that he would pursue his point. It was unthinkable that I would go back to Belfast in a dress. That evening I left the ashram and walked out along the riverside. I jogged from one end of the promenade to the other a number of times, and at each end I jumped up and down briskly to shake off the lassitude in my bones. Then I went back to my room to meditate. In the morning I went again to

Grindlay's bank in Chandni Chowk to ask if the money had arrived, and they told me again it had not. Walking home, I felt horribly tired and weak. A little girl looked up at me then screamed and ran away. By the time I reached the ashram, I was exhausted, and aching in almost every part of my body. I collapsed onto my bed.

When Satya Shankar brought me lunch, I told him I could not eat it, and he reported to Swamiji that I was unwell. Swamiji called to me and I went out to explain to him how I felt. I could hardly stand. He said that I was jaundiced about the eyes and neck. I had already surmised from the discoloration of my urine and the dull ache, like the smart from a punch below my rib cage, that I had hepatitis. I could do nothing now but lie still, with my whole body feeling like an encumbrance. In the morning I was able to walk with Satya Shankar to a doctor, for an injection, some pills and advice on diet. In two or three days I was feeling stronger, though I had to observe the diet for about six weeks. Swamiji put no strain of work on me while I was recovering, but one morning he called me to him and told me that he would be leaving to hold a *yagna* – a sacrifice – near his hometown of Ettawa.

A *yagna* is a festive occasion. The centrepiece is the offering of foodstuffs, chiefly rice and ghee, into a fire constructed according to a strict Vedic prescription governing the number of bricks and the pattern of their layout. There are various recommended *yagnas*. Some are for specific ends: prosperity, the birth of a son, the welfare of the nation. I did not enquire deeply into this one. I sensed it was something we would argue over. Swamiji said he expected a very large number of people to attend. He had invited a couple of cabinet ministers he had known years before, including Atal Behari Vajpayee, who later became the prime minister of India who ordered nuclear tests to demonstrate his power to Pakistan. I think Swamiji would have approved of that.

I offered him my opinion, based on the reading of newspapers, that they would be unlikely to come, because they would be exposing themselves to the charge that they were fanatical Hindus who cared more for feeding the gods than feeding their people. Swamiji surprised me and said he saw sense in this argument. Presumably he wanted to pick his own moment for a quarrel. He asked me if I would make a speech at the *yagna* in praise of Hinduism. I said I would.

I returned to my room to think over what I would do. I trawled some ideas but did not yet commit them to paper. That afternoon I went into the centre of Delhi to buy books, and as I travelled back to the ashram I realised that I was quite elated, probably because I could see the conflict coming to a head. A part of me relished that conflict with all its uncertainty and all its promise of change. As soon as I got back to my room, I started working on a speech. What I wrote presented no conflict with Swamiji's ideas. It was a reflection on the differences between Hinduism and Christianity, saying that I thought that the religious conception of the universe was enriched by notions of reincarnation and karma. I confined myself to this subject, without touching on social structures, divine incarnation or revelation.

The next day, Swamiji mentioned the planned *yagna* again, and I told him that I had written a speech and that I could show it to him. He interjected to say that he wanted me to concentrate on praising the *Varna* system, the system that divides Hindu society in four. My heart sank. I said I could not do that. He snapped at me. 'What have you been reading?'

He challenged me to write a criticism of the *Varna* system and said he would show me point for point where I was wrong, and whenever I tried to reason he simply repeated this challenge. 'Do not fight with me. Do you think you are wiser than me? I will discard you.'

I sat there quietly, internally disengaging myself from every possible spontaneous reaction. This was too serious. It would take time to assimilate. I surrendered all will to fight him, though I was determined not to concede my point and not to agree to his request. I said: 'You know I trust your guidance in meditation, and you know that religion for me, as you have always said it should be, is founded on experience and not tradition.'

But he sat silently, ignoring me. After a few moments of this, I rose and walked away. Next morning, Satya Shankar came to my room. He was standing nervously in the doorway, looking dejected. He said: 'Swamiji has sent me to take away all the work that you have.'

I had some maps of the Brig Ghat construction site, some architectural diagrams. I had copies of the *Gita* commentary and I had an unfinished manuscript of the book I had been writing about Swamiji. I handed these to Satya Shankar, but held onto one copy of the manuscript. He asked me for the folders but I told him I was keeping them. I still had hopes that these jobs might one day be finished.

'Swamiji may want them.'

'Then Swamiji will come for them.' Poor Satya Shankar. He was frightened.

'You should not fight with Swamiji.'

'It is not my will to fight with Swamiji.' But he seemed not to understand that. He was having to subject himself every day to greater humiliation than was being demanded of me, and his survival depended on it. For me to upset the whole atmosphere of the ashram over an assertion of independence just seemed like an indulgence to him.

Swamiji did not call me that day. That night I lay out in front of my room, my mind strung taut with apprehension. He would be leaving in the morning for the *yagna*, and he would be away for a month. I skirted the edge of sleep and had troubled dreams. I was awake with the dawn, and watched him come out of his room with his trunks, watched the gates open and the taxi arrive, but I made no move to approach him, and he went without a word, and offered no blessing.

'Swamiji is very angry with you,' Satya Shankar said.

'Swamiji is a yogi. He is not supposed to get angry.'

'You should not fight with Swamiji.'

'Swamiji should not fight with me.' That sounded like arrogance.

'Usually Swamiji leaves money for food for you when he goes away, but this time he has left none. There is only flour and dahl.'

'Is that all the food we have for a whole month?'

'That is all. I think Swamiji is very angry.'

I had no money. I had been going periodically to the bank to try to withdraw a sum which Walter said he had sent, but the cashier told me every time that it had not arrived. I had been on a light diet for weeks, because of my hepatitis, and I was weak. I thought that the only hope of avoiding malnutrition now was to get that money and buy proper food. The bank continued to insist it had nothing for me. Then a man called Ram Gopal came to the ashram, and stayed for the whole month of Swamiji's absence. He based himself there while looking for work. Ram Gopal fed us. I enjoyed that month. I could walk out the gate without consulting anyone, and I could live at ease in the ashram without feeling the shadow of Swamiji's mind leaning ponderously and inquisitively over everything I did.

The weather in Delhi in April is hot but not humid. The mornings and evenings are pleasant times to walk along the river or out through the bazaar. The scourge of my nights was the mosquitoes; some of the afternoons, when we took a siesta, were pure torment, when the electricity was cut and we couldn't use the fans. In a month or two, life would be even more uncomfortable, and all work would stop, but I would acclimatise myself to that eventually, just as I was acclimatising myself to this dry heat. Satya Shankar and the visitor, Ram Gopal, were my closest companions that month. Ram Gopal was about my own age and he spoke good English and we enjoyed conversation, often sitting in the evening for hours, comparing life in the east with life in the west.

Satya Shankar was more mischievous, freed also from Swamiji's authority for a while. He would take out the musical instruments that were used for worship and play them and sing through the afternoons. He would be wild and boisterous with other boys who came to visit. They wrestled on the lawn. Swamiji had proposed that I keep a distance from people and not engage in their play, and I tried to go along with this. I would laugh and joke with the boys, but I would shun them like a pert snob when they were more raucous, and I asked them to be quieter in the mornings and evenings, at the times I had set aside for meditation.

Swamiji returned to Delhi at the end of May, but he did not speak to me, and I made no approach to him either. On the second day after his arrival, Satya Shankar came to me and told me that he had orders to lock the back door of my room. This led out into an area which had been used as a kitchen, and was now a store room for building materials. There was a convenient water tap there. Presumably my use of this tap had defiled it. A bathroom at the other corner of the ashram grounds had been specifically built for me so that I would not have to trespass on reserved ground like this. This decision to bar my access to the water tap seemed calculated to insult me. I let Satya Shankar into my room and he locked the door. He stopped on the way out again, and showed me a dejected, hangdog face.

'Mr Malky, I think you had better leave. Swamiji is very angry with you. You should write to your friends in Germany and ask them to bring you home.' I concentrated on quelling the disheartening effect of his words. They were, after all, only his words. Swamiji had said nothing.

I had befriended Mr Shanker, the man Gerlinde had stayed with. He had been at college with Swamiji and often visited the ashram. To me he was Shankerji. It puzzled me that Shankerji paid respect to Swamiji because he seemed more secular in his thinking than anyone else close to him. Perhaps he was just studying the ashram for a paper he planned to write. He also had an Alsatian dog at his home and Swamiji regarded dogs as dirty. Shankerji's dog was vegetarian but one day I saw it attack and kill a rat at his home. I liked Shankerji and we would talk sometimes for hours, yet there was often something like a blush clouding his dealings with me. Perhaps I was too candid with him. He was helpful to me and later introduced me to the editor of *The Hindustan Times* who invited me to write articles and short stories in the last year I spent in India.

I spoke to Shankerji at his home about the problem with Swamiji. He advised me to approach Swamiji and start a discussion. He felt I was being unnecessarily intransigent.

'It's all very well to say that,' I said, 'but Swamiji's idea of discussing a thing is that I should submit to learning from him, on the understanding that, in the end, I will agree with him. That's not a discussion. I'm sure you don't treat your students like that. Swamiji thinks I hate the *Varna* system, but I don't. It's really none of my business. It's certainly not my job to persuade Hindus to follow it, when many of them do hate it.'

I felt that if I approached Swamiji, I might provoke a hostile reaction, so I applied the same kind of indifference to him as he applied to me. That, of course, led to stalemate. Then my money problem was solved. I had received an assurance from the Bombay branch of Grindlay's that money had been forwarded to me in Delhi, and I took the letter to the clerk who had been insisting all along that he had nothing for me. It turned out that he had been checking his list against the M of Malachi rather than the O of O'Doherty. Now I could afford to move out of the ashram, stay in a hotel and arrange to go back to Europe, but I didn't want to do that. I wanted to continue with my *sadhana*, and even though I had gone weeks without even talking to Swamiji, I was still meditating every day, for at least an hour each morning and night.

A certain intransigence and rebelliousness are almost natural to me. I can be strong-headed and stubborn and enjoy being strong-headed and stubborn, so I decided to examine my own thought processes as thoroughly as I could, to understand how much I was being driven by impulses that were not declaring themselves. I decided to try posing embarrassing and challenging questions to myself because part of me was enjoying this titanic struggle. In my notebook I re-examined all the stages leading up to the conflict, and I tried to assess my own behaviour objectively. When Swamiji had raised the question of my wearing a robe I had gone away a little exhilarated, not because I thought I might agree with him, but because secretly I relished the clash with him. It seemed suspicious to me that I had anticipated the moments of tension between me and Swamiji, if not the actual issues that would divide us. I had seen storms rising, or I had smelled them on the wind. The clash had not surprised me when it came. Now it seemed to me that I had wanted a showdown with Swamiji and had prepared in advance for it.

I looked back at other periods in my life in which relationships had come to an end, or I had left where I was living – my resignation from a job or my sacking from another – and I questioned my own versions of these events. I began to see myself as a perpetual avoider, motivated in part by mischief and in part by fear of commitment, and I went further back in my memory to see if I could find out what had made me like that. I asked myself if I had really left Ireland and my job in journalism because I was confused by war or because I had simply baulked at the workload and professional responsibility. I asked myself if I had squandered my studies and a chance at university for the same reason. Had I failed with Linda simply because I couldn't bear to close down the option of walking away and trying something else? Would it have been more brave to have stayed with her than to come here?

This self-interrogation was disheartening and I had no way to bolster my morale while I was doing it. The whole point was to embrace doubt and accept regret, not to explain myself more reassuringly. I began to feel empty and guilty, and I accepted that even if I was right to refuse to be manipulated by Swamiji into making speeches I didn't believe, I was still the sort of person who would relish this type of conflict.

I began to examine my dreams. The nights were humid and my sleep was patchy and light, so dreams were closer to the surface and easier to grasp. I would roll out my sleeping bag on a concrete surface and lie flat on my back on top of it. I would place a notebook and a pen within reach, and before I went to sleep I would frame a mental resolve to observe my dreams closely and wake to record them before they slipped away. This worked well. As soon as I started to write the account of a dream, I would begin to remember one that had preceded it, and then another before that. It was normal to end up with a chain of five dreams, when I had started out consciously recalling only one.

Now I look back through my diaries and find the meaning of a dream obvious, and I am appalled at how little I understood it at the time. It shows that my self-analysis was poor and I was enmeshed in evasions about what was actually going on in my relationship with Swamiji. This dream work was also exhausting and depressing. I think now that those dreams were efforts by my subconscious mind to strengthen and reassure me, though, failing to see this at the time, I confused myself further. The loss of sleep, owing to the heat and humidity, would have been tiring enough, but it was worsened by my nervous restlessness. What little sleep I did get was diluted by my efforts to remain self-conscious. I was allowing my brain no rest at all.

Shankerji visited the ashram one day. He had had a long conversation with Swamiji and then came to my room. He conveyed to me Swamiji's sense that I had a pre-set resistance to believing in the Varna system. I admitted that I had. Having grown up in an educational and social milieu where democracy and civil rights were much discussed, I resisted teachings that contradicted those values. But why did I hesitate to make the case for those values? Only because the wrangling would be tedious and I knew already that we would never agree. But did that mean I didn't have confidence in what I believed, or in myself? I should be mature enough to reason through this, as ready to reach one conclusion as the other, relying on logic alone. I was confused. What part of my resistance was reason and what part reaction?

I imagined myself going home to Ireland and suggesting that society be divided in four, that people only be allowed to inter-marry within their class or section of society, and that the labouring people should not be allowed to use the same sources of drinking water as the rest of us. Was Swamiji mad to think that I could be coaxed into viewing the world in such a way? Was I a coward to resolve in advance that even if I was persuaded of the truth of his teaching that I would keep quiet about it?

'No,' he had said. 'It is too late to save the west, but if you think about it with an open mind you will see that we have something very precious here in India.'

I said to Shankerji: 'It is very difficult for me to consider that a system that embraces ideas of racial purity, arranged marriage, untouchability – that this could be right. And even if I did consider it seriously, then knowing the perversity of the mind as I am coming to know it, I would never wholly trust my conclusions.'

'Then you can't trust your conclusions about anything.'

'Perhaps not.'

What I was really afraid of was that Swamiji would talk me in stages through to a conclusion in favour of the *Varna* system and at the end, if I was to restore my integrity, I would have to un-pick again the sequence of ideas that I had agreed to. This was too much work. I had been through Northern Ireland where it mattered unreasonably whether you were a Catholic or a Protestant – something you had no choice in – and I had left in part because I resented that. Now I was being asked to say that people should be labelled more thoroughly even than that, that their destiny should be fixed within a social order, and they could be told what work was appropriate for them, and from what group they might choose their spouses. I felt strongly and spontaneously, without reflection, that all of this was repulsive, but my spontaneity in it-self made my conclusion suspect. I hadn't thought it through. That was ahead of me, and I resented that I should have to deal with it.

I began to feel like a beetle in a jar being taunted with a stick.

Meanwhile, I continued to observe my dreams. Some seemed to create a possible future in which I would regret that I had not wholly committed myself to a monastic life. Some dramatised the fear of separation from the body in imagery like a 1950s science fiction film. One seems to have been a precognitive vision of a minor incident. I had occasional dreams of almost incredible lucidity. In my room in Delhi one afternoon, I lay sleeping on the bed. Suddenly I was in a room surrounded by big cardboard boxes. I had to lift and stack them away from the door to find my way out. This was a dream, but I was awake, making mental observations about the experience itself. I could even see my actual right forearm draped across my face as it was where I lay on the bed. I got out of the room, and I was standing at the head of a valley. The view was finely detailed and the bright summer colours had a granular texture. An imp with long black hair tried to draw me down into the valley. I worked out that he was trying to woo me towards the edge of a very steep slope to push me over. I can see now that this imp was Swamiji, as my secret self depicted him, but that did not even occur to me until years later.

I had often since puberty seen images very clearly before sleep, but though I had read of lucid dreaming, I had never experienced it as clearly as this before, nor have I since.

After a few more days, my buoyancy and cheerfulness returned to me, not I think, because I had learned anything from my dream analysis or self-examination, but just because I had some underlying reserve of energy which could not be wholly repressed. On Shankerji's next visit, I was exercising on the veranda outside my room. We talked, and this time there was not the same cloud of tension and apprehension over me. I was able to consider his suggestions. Swamiji was sitting at the other side of the lawn, alone and reading a book. Shankerji had told him, I think, that he would try to bring me to him. 'Come with me now,' he said. 'We will go over to Swamiji. What is the harm? We can talk it over and you need not feel afraid, for I will be there, and if he is unreasonable, I will support you.'

'No,' I said. 'I will go to him, but I will go in my own time and alone, just when I feel in the right mood for it.'

In the morning, when Swamiji came out to sit in the shade I went straight to him and said: 'I have come to ask you to clarify my position here in the ashram.'

'Very well.' He called to Satya Shankar, who was washing pots at the pump, and asked him to bring out a reed mat for me to sit on. I sat close to his feet. I was wearing a pair of white pyjama pants made of rough cotton.

Swamiji said: 'How do you feel?'

'I feel well and strong.'

'Do you know what this cloth is?' I took a fold of it between my fingers and scanned my memory for its Indian name. As I was concentrating on this, I began to feel a painful poking sensation through the lower vertebrae, as if a ghastly, relentless finger was probing them. 'How do you feel?' said Swamiji. I knew that if I told him about this nervous reaction, he would take the credit for causing it. The only way to keep open, for the moment, the idea that he was not actually doing this himself by psychic power, was to pretend that it was not happening.

'I am perfectly well,' I said. 'I am feeling strong and confident.'

'But physically? How do you feel physically?'

'I feel perfectly all right. There is no discomfort. The hepatitis has passed. I am bearing the heat well. I am getting used to it.'

After about half a minute the painful prodding sensation abated.

Swamiji said: 'What clarification do you think is necessary?'

'You have been back from the *yagna* for a month now, and in this time there has been no communication between us. It seems I am no longer required here.'

'You have been troubling yourself for no reason at all, and suffering depression when you might have come to me and spoken to me and not let your imagination trouble you like this.'

'I hardly feel that it was wrong of me to judge things as I did.'

He chuckled, with a little effort: 'That is all right. It is for the disciple to be wrong and the guru to be right. Otherwise, there would be no need for the relationship between them.'

He was not going to come to the point, unless I insisted on discussing it. He was going to let the real quarrel pass.

I said: 'You asked me to speak on the *Varna* system, and I told you that I would not do that. Since then we have been estranged.'

'We will be able to talk these things over in time, and you will understand them better. But, for the meantime, it is good that the air is clear. You will not be bothering yourself like this again.'

I chose to be more specific. 'I do not feel at ease, entering into discussion with you on the *Varna* system, or on anything else, if it is emphatically a condition of that discussion that in the end I will agree with you.'

'There is no condition other than a willingness to increase your understanding. Without this willingness, how can any of us advance in life?'

I felt that he was too strong for me, that I would never trust myself not to be manipulated by him, that I would be sure of my own thinking only when I was away from him. He said: 'Try to see things from my point of view. Do not harden your heart against me. Increase your receptivity, and don't be a slave to spontaneous resistance born out of past habits.'

We deferred the crisis, but I looked ahead to the day when I would leave him, and I knew that I would go feeling as guilty as he could make me feel. He would see me as acting out of personal defiance, ignorance and ingratitude, and I would be condemned to wondering for years after I left if this was not really how it was.

PART THREE

I was in Geneva when I heard that Swamiji had died. This was in
1982, and I was living with Véronique in her flat in St Jean, overlooking the Rhône. I was thirty-one years old and going to school
every day in Palais Wilson, the old League of Nations Building, learning to teach English as a foreign language, in preparation for a job
in Libya, where my pupils would be Air Defence Force cadets, but
that's another story.

I was still a bit of a yogi then. Véronique would burn with exasperation if she came home from work to find me in my underpants
standing on my head in the middle of her living-room, as if I had
nothing better to do.

German friends of mine had had news from the daughter of
friends of theirs, who had been to India looking for Swamiji. The
girls had called at the little garden ashram in Nigambodh Marg,
by the ring road, just south of the Interstate Bus Station, and someone there had told them that he was dead. I imagined white-hair-
ed Mooneemji from the cow shelter next door fussing round the
visitors, trying to give them the details in Hindi and patchy English, and then perhaps Savita, waiting her turn to speak, deferring
first to her father, then explaining the whole thing in the fuller
English she had part-learned at school and part from me.

I wept. I had lost something dear, but what had I lost, a man
I had not spoken to for three years? Véronique was bewildered. I
had told her already that I had lived in India, under a guru and that
I had come away to be a westerner again. She was charmed by the
story. She teased me that I walked like an Indian. She was amazed
that on the first day we met, in Donegal, we talked about her own
Indian forebears on her mother's side, the Sens.

'Are you related to Keshab Chunder Sen?' She had never in
her life met anyone who had heard of Keshab Chunder Sen until
we talked about nineteenth century Bengal in an Irish country pub.
But she thought that Swamiji was part of a past I had broken away
from.

What I felt I lost that day was not a living relationship with

Swamiji but the chance to go back someday and explain myself to him, after I had worked out what pattern there was to my life. I had been, for a time, a devout and attentive yogi, celibate but for one lapse and one leap. I had now put that behind me. Yet I had believed.

What I lost when I learned that Swamiji was dead was the security of knowing that some day I could go back to him and sit before him in his cottage in the ashram garden, perhaps accompanied by a wife, with my life in order. I had lost the chance to tell him what I was doing and explain to him that it had been worth leaving the path of *sadhana* to find it.

I would have been able to tell him, had he lived, that after Geneva and Libya I got to make a living out of my questions when I became a journalist, working in Religious Affairs, in Northern Ireland, the tetchiest religious environment in Europe. I would have liked him to see me as a grown man confident of the decision I had made to leave him. I would have told him more about the religion my mind had been framed in before I met him, that I had spiritual roots in Ireland that simply could not be transplanted in India, and that it was here that the only Path I was really called to had to be walked.

I grew up in a fundamentalist faith. What strikes me on reflection is that in going to Swamiji I was trying to find an environment in which my religious inclinations might function more comfortably. This monastic life just happened to be a different faith with different lunatics in charge. I gave Swamiji his power over me; I allowed myself to believe that he was superhuman, which is what a parent is to a child, a guard to a prisoner. And my sojourn there was not a silly waste of time, but an experience I had to have, and was unable to avoid.

Swamiji, however, did not want me to have an experience, or at least not a learning experience; not an interaction with people which leaves you wiser about yourself. What he offered was a spiritual experience through meditation, obedience, celibacy. He thought that psychological growth and the spiritual quest were two different things. When I suggested occasionally that I might learn more about myself from experience out in the world, he said: 'Why not learn through the experience of others?'

This sums up the instruction of all churches: don't live, just take our word for it that the world is full of pain and that we have the formula for circumventing that pain. His understanding of the law of karma – the effect of what you have done in past lifetimes on what you experience now – was that it described a wholly mechanistic trap that only the grace of God could yank you out of. The idea that experience itself might make you wiser was only relevant to him as a worldly truth; worldly wisdom provided nothing to open the portals to the spirit's freedom from rebirth; it just led to finding different, perhaps more practical, ways of managing the world you were trapped in. Better to walk away from the trap. He believed that someone like me, a twenty-five-year-old boy, could break the bonds with the world and turn his attention to meditation and become an enlightened yogi, without ever solving the problems presented to him by experience – and inexperience – like why he seemed determined to replicate the confusion of his own childhood.

'So,' he might have said, 'you think you are driven by the conditioning of one lifetime and need to sort that out; really you are driven by the conditioning of a billion lifetimes – since you were an insect. Why add to that?'

Even when I was most absorbed in Swamiji and in meditation, I always, from a reserved part of my thinking, resisted what he wanted for me. Emer's instruction to Cuhoolin in William Larminie's poem, *Fand*, made more sense to me than the simple injunction to turn my back on something called the world. Emer is the earthly woman contending with the lure of the Goddess, telling her man that he belongs with her and has a life to live. She pleads with Cuhoolin not to fall in love with a goddess until he has filled himself with life and can bear the steady unchanging gaze:

Wait till thou hast sea-depths –
Till all the tides of life and deed,
Of action and of meditation,
Of service unto others and their love,
Shall pour into the caverns of thy being
The might of their unconquerable floods.
Then canst thou bear the glow of eyes divine ...

By this logic the yogi withdrawing to a cave for meditation would be wasting his time if he hadn't completed himself in experience of life first. It made sense. Could a Buddhist accept, on the word of another, the Four Noble Truths that said that all life was suffering and that suffering could be escaped by ignoring the world? The Buddhist would have to be convinced intellectually of the emptiness of life, so that no mere recovery of the spirits would unhinge a commitment.

I left the ashram. I had to fight to tear myself away from Swamiji after three years. I had been going along with a view of life that excluded all considerations of wilful self-interest; now I had changed my mind. When I went to him to tell him my decision, I could hardly speak the words. I took care not to look into his eyes. I had to write down all my points and make them like a child reading an exercise to a teacher. We agreed that I would work another six months with him to finish the commentary on the *Gita*. During that period he insisted on intensive discussion on all the points we disagreed on, the divine origins of scripture, the incarnations of God, the *Varna* system, the sanctity of the cow, everything. This turned absurd. We would walk up and down along the promenade by the river exhausting the question of whether God had incarnated. His proof, in the end, was that the scriptures had said so, and since the scriptures were true – he said they were one of the 'valid means of cognition' – then God had incarnated. What had I to offer – he demanded – that outweighed the authority of a truth that had been accepted for thousands of years?

He did not regard the teaching of the *Vedanta* as a folk tradition but as a precise body of knowledge. It was a school. He had no doubt that Vedic history went back beyond the time of the Indus Valley civilisation at Mohenjo Daro. He believed in the literal truth of the Vedic scriptures, and other sacred texts. Lord Krishna really was God. He had indeed been the charioteer of Arjuna at the battle of Kurukshetra, and really had paused before the clash of armies to explain the meaning of life and destiny.

What this was really all about was the waning of the small man's adoration of the big man. Why do we men sometimes wilt like adoring fans before a strong man who elects not to squash us? Why do we sometimes feel that the flattery entailed in the simple withdrawal of threat is more than is conceivably deserved? Adulation is the other side of fear. Fascination is the other side of suspicion.

I grew up thinking that my father was a good man because his anger passed quickly. The truth is that he had irrational rages every day of his life, but whenever he was angry with me, I always blamed myself, and when his rage subsided, I felt forgiven, and grateful to be forgiven.

You can grow strong in the shadow of a strong man who allows you to regress to an undefensive innocence and to rehearse your power on him. He may provide a great service; he cannot expect to be thanked for it. If he then acts the master one day longer than you allow, you reject him. In the end it was down to this: I believed what I wanted to believe, and I wanted to believe in what would allow me to go.

I did give myself for a time to a life of devotion and intense meditation, enough to be engaged and enraptured and humiliated and overawed, and even appalled. I came back from that, clear in my mind that the price of further engagement was the death of my personality, whether in profound entrancement or in surrender to Swamiji, and neither was an option. Indeed there was something like a spiritual experience motivating me to go.

One day, before my decision to leave had crystallised, I was walking along the Ganges when I noticed a new box-shaped thatch shelter that had been built on the far side. Probably some hermit had set up home there, or maybe a *chai walla*, a tea-seller, who did not know that the pilgrims gathered on this side. I was staring across, trying to focus through the sparkling glare when Vajpayee, our cook came up and distracted me. I turned to him and he was standing crouched and wrapped in his old woollen blanket and smiling. He looked frail and dilapidated but oblivious of the hardship of his life. I could not have endured being as poor as he was and having to work as hard, and particularly having to bear the close attention of Swamiji to every detail of my life. I was in a relaxed unproblematic mood, content – I don't know why – to believe that things would always be as they were and that they were all right. I was finding that my heart would open, without meditation, without the comfort of Swamiji's approval, and that I could love without fear.

Perhaps it was the sudden shift of my mind from searching

concentration across the river to passive attention to the man beside me, but there was a sudden swing to levity. In that moment I seemed to feel the quality of my whole life in front of me, a sense of it all having a dependable familiar and friendly texture. I was fit and at ease. There was an anchorage for me, as sure as the river and the sun. I seemed able to appreciate my life for once as a fixed knowable quantum. I had no need to be hiding from the future, from work and from relationships and challenges. I had no need to immerse myself in the contemplation of God; I had only to live the portion that was given me.

There is a negative version of that moment of contentment, I know. However happy you are now, you will again face disappointment and loneliness and the return of the clear-headed conviction that life is empty. I have wondered sometimes if that isn't qualitatively a clearer, more dependable insight. Perhaps what I was intuiting was that there was a fixed balance of joy and despair in my life that would not change whatever I did. In fact, I vacillated for months over whether or not to go home, and I did not retain the insight of that day clearly enough to depend on it. I was hung up on my commitment to surrender to the will of God. I wanted to be shown what to do, not to have to decide. I stayed on until I had exhausted the expectation that I might evade a clear personal choice and saw that there was no escape from making a decision. Then I chose to leave.

I had been in a calmer phase in my last summer there, and my meditation was steadier and deeper. In that calmness a simple undramatic thing had happened: a white disc appeared in front of me during my sitting and absorbed my full attention. I felt I had the option to stay with this and discard my whole personality or hold back and remain the person I was. I was no more able to go into that than I would have been able to jump off a cliff. I had a life to live. You die to yourself, to live to the Other, but if you are not ready, then simply, you are not ready.

There was another strange coincidence in those last weeks. I met a German man who called himself Shanti. He was also meditating. He told me that he used a pocket Bible as an oracle. When he wanted to make a decision, he would choose a page at random, dip in a finger and read a line for advice. He told me that St Augustine was converted to Christianity when he opened a Bible at random and read: 'Not in rioting and drunkenness, not in chambering and impurities, not in contention and envy, but put ye on the Lord Jesus Christ and make not provision for the flesh in all its concupiscences.'

I tried the same thing and I got a message very unlike the one Augustine got. I read: 'Go thy way; eat thy bread with joy and drink thy wine with a merry heart, for the Lord now accepts your works.'

There were times then and since, when the world seemed to respond as did the world of dreams: with meaning. This is the fringe of madness in our culture, not a desirable state to be in nor one from which it is easy to communicate experience to others. But sometimes you have to laugh.

At night I would watch the lizards on my ceiling picking off the mosquitoes until their black, filled bellies showed through their translucent flesh, and they fell bloated to the floor. In the morning the dead mosquitoes lay like a film of dust for me to sweep out into the garden. This was a summer of astonishing thunderstorms and flooding, but there were warm nights when I could comfortably sit out under a tree. I began to relax in the evenings chatting to Satya Shankar and the others.

'Mr Malky,' said Satya Shankar one evening after dinner, 'tell us how to make some money.'

I looked around at the empty rooms and I had an idea. I joked that we could rent space to the hippy tourists. Swamiji was to be away for weeks. He would never know. We laughed and toyed with the idea and then reluctantly agreed that we wouldn't do it, but when I went back to my room I wrote a short story based on that idea. I played out all the mischief that I could imagine. I typed up the story and sent it off to *The Illustrated Weekly of India* in Bombay. A week later they accepted it for publication. That started me working as a writer. I wrote other short stories for *The Hindustan Times*. One was about a man living in an ashram who wonders if the teenage girl who brings his food in the evening is developing a crush on him. He contemplates giving her a little kiss when next he finds himself alone with her, in that uncertain moment, as they wait for something to happen and before they shake themselves back into their routine lives. I called it, 'What are you Looking at, Mr Joe?'

I was soon writing for a living, though a modest one. I made an arrangement with the editor of *The Hindustan Times* that he would pay me when I delivered a story to him, rather than a month or more after publication, which is the normal practice. So if I was broke, I could write a story and take it straight to him. That would have been a simple way to live if I could have sustained it, but I would need accommodation when I left the ashram and I would not be able to afford that.

In my last weeks in India I stayed in tourist hotels and travelled to the mountains. I met girls and made a fool of myself since I had not had that comfort for years. One night on a veranda in a hill station during a thunderstorm, watching the banks of mist come over the jungle I shared my contentment with a German girl, whose name I don't even remember now. I said: 'You know, right now I feel this is where I am meant to be.'

She said: 'That is exactly how I feel myself, as if this moment is ordained.'

'In that case, it must be ordained that we be here together.'

'I don't think so,' she said.

My period of celibacy was over now. I had not made my break with Swamiji to free myself for sex. He had engaged my heart as much as any woman had, and he lost it. It was not because I needed to love a woman but because I needed to be free to think. But it wasn't long after making the break that I began to dwell on the new possibilities. I looked around Delhi for women of about my own age and compared myself to them. They were all, of course, four of five years older than the women I had been with before, apart from Gerlinde. They were grown up women, not girls. This struck me as an amazing discovery. I watched Julie who was twenty-six enter the travel agent where I was buying my ticket. We went for a cup of tea. She was Australian. We lay out all night on the embankment by the river.

My first conscious orgasms, after years of abstinence, were loud and convulsive, pure delight, but I lost friendships because of my urgency. I could, in reflective moments, remember all that Swamiji had warned me about lust and concede that it was indeed a problem. I had learned nothing about sex in the years in the ashram and came out like a clumsy adolescent.

A week before I left India I visited Swamiji at the ashram again. He was ill. I didn't know how ill. He had been to the hospital for tests, having found blood in his urine. It had been a horrific ordeal for him. I was not accustomed to him sharing his fears with me and I did not know how to accept them.

He said: 'I had to come back in a taxi and you know it is my rule not to touch the ordinary people, but people were sitting right next to me, rubbing against me.' The distaste showed in the curl of his lip. What should I have said? 'Poor Swamiji, if only you could allow yourself to be ordinary too.' I said nothing.

I went back to Ireland after seven years away, three in England, four in India. I tried to retain some of the sensitivity of meditation and some of the emotional candour which I had found, but this was challenged every day. A simple thing. One day I left my parent's house in Andersonstown for a trip to Donegal, dressed in a loose frock shirt, one of my Indian *khador kurtas*. A boy sneered at me: 'Hey missus!'

I still, for a time, thought of myself as someone who had achieved spiritual insights and experience and who was still on a spiritual journey. I was also experiencing after-effects from the years of intensive meditation, flying dreams, electrical aura sensations, sometimes in the middle of the night, sometimes in tiring or stressful situations. What I needed in that time was to learn to identify my own emotions and sensations and to relate them to the things that occasioned them, and to escape from a habit of imagining them to be spiritually meaningful, to reject every delusional impression of grace on the understanding that a real spiritual event would survive the scepticism anyway. I had to peel religion off me like a clammy web and learn to accept the actual life I was living.

I came to feel that the inevitability of disappointment was the familiar part of everything, that it was good to be an ordinary, flawed human.

The culture shock was in coming home and having to dismantle my sense of mission and vocation and accepting ordinariness. There were times during that transition when I felt music inside me rising and threatening to sweep me away, that's how vulnerable I was. At times my nerves sang with stress and distress. When that stage passed, and I learned to manage life as a grounding of my nerves rather than as a stretching of them, I became a happier person. This changed the way I wrote, allowed me to be a happy journalist rather than a fretful poet.

I do not have the intelligence to rationalise and obviate every impression, but in trying I have dismantled gods. And that is what the Upanishads told me to do, to dismiss everything that seems it may be God with, 'Not this, Not this', to trust only to the possibility of God being in what's left when everything conceivable is rejected.

I lived a disconnected life, journalism being the main thread through it, and I learned more about my psychological inheritance than I would have done as a monk, and I resolved some of my destructive contradictions. I met Véronique and lived in Geneva. I trained as a language instructor and went to Libya and worked with young conscripts and gave them Belfast accents. I fought with men. I had relationships that broke up and broke me. Would I have been able to leapfrog over all that this taught me through meditation and prayer? I do not believe so. I am one of those who, loving life, shall lose it. I cannot die to the world to save my soul.

The last I heard of Swamiji was two years after I left. I had had an intimation that he was dead, a dream in which he showed me his hand with a black cross drawn in the palm. This settled for me the question of whether I would go back again and explain my life to him. I wept like a little boy for about half an hour on Véronique's kitchen table, and then I dried my tears and let go of him.

I visited Gerlinde three times in Austria. The first time, she was still the woman I had known. She had a lovely big apartment in Linz and lived with her daughters across the street from the school where Hitler and Wittgenstein had studied as children. She showed me the family album, with a picture of herself as a little child in a frock playing before a wooden house in the countryside in wartime. Her father was not there. He had volunteered for the Russian front and never came home. I did my *asanas* in a bedroom there and her cat Gwendolina shat on my sleeping bag. I met her boyfriend Christian, and her previous boyfriend, Rheinhold, who was still close. He was an astrologer now and drew up a chart for me. They drove me round Upper Austria and showed me the amazing wood-carved altar in the church at Fredericksberg. I parted with them at the German border and hitch-hiked home.

A year later, when I was back in Linz, I was looking for a girlfriend and hugged Gerlinde too close and annoyed her. When she had wanted me, I had brushed her off. When I wanted her, she brushed me off. She looked overshadowed now. She was living like a lodger in her own home. She let her daughters use most of the space. She had even given her car to the boyfriend of one of them. I said I thought they were using her. She was contemptuous of that materialistic way of thinking. She was working with a print artist called Fritz on a book about Linz, *The Linz Egg*. Fritz clearly didn't like me. Gerlinde explained that she and he struggled and argued, and out of the tension came the creative energy to write the book. It was his way of working.

Two years after that she was living in Vienna and writing a play. She showed me the palaces and the cafes and took me to the theatre. She was wearing gloves all the time, and in the theatre she booked an empty seat beside her. I didn't know it then, but she had started carrying a gun. She vacillated between being affection-ate and disdainful, and asked me to move out after four days. I stay-ed a few days in Christian's flat then took the night train to Geneva.

Gerlinde and I laughed and played when we were together, but she was frequently overtaken with an exasperation which would be as likely to focus on me as on anybody. Her paradox was that she was both strong and vulnerable. She had been dominated by men; it was the main focus of her writing. She hated herself for having been dominated by them. She would seek love as a giddy little girl, then shrug that off and scowl at anyone who treated her in such a way.

We wrote to each other a few times after that and spoke on the phone. I would be struggling to make a living as a freelance journalist and she would counsel me not to worry about money. 'So long as you can plan three months ahead, that is enough,' she said. That was the position she was in. She had enough savings to last another three months.

My problem was that I wanted to write out of my own ex-perience and imagination, rather than according to prescription. I had had occasional jobs as a reporter and I had not done well or been happy. I had to find my own path into journalism. When I got trapped in the toilet for the disabled on the Larne boat, com-ing home from that last trip to Vienna, I found a story to write.

It happened like this: I could not open the toilet door from the inside. I found a switch marked Alarm beside the toilet bowl.

I pressed it and a light came on above the door on the inside but no one came. Perhaps if I switched it on and off ... ? But the switch had only one function, to switch that light on.

I had guessed already that this would make a yarn, to tell if not to sell. It got better. I stood up on the toilet bowl, propped one foot against the heavy sliding door and leaned forward to inspect the alarm light. There was a switch there too. This one only switched the light off. I climbed down and turned the light on again with the switch at the toilet bowl, and climbed up again onto the toilet bowl, balanced myself with a foot against the door and reached up and turned it off.

I scrambled back and forth between the two switches, to flash the light and create a signal. Eventually a man on the other side of the door shouted in: 'Do you need help?'

He wrestled with the door, then said he'd go and find others. 'Don't panic.' I didn't.

When three men on the outside finally yanked the jammed door open, one of them looked at me and said sternly, as if I'd been wasting his time: 'You're not disabled.'

And another, reading the broader implications of the problem, said: 'Now, isn't it as well he's not.'

I got twenty pounds for that story and it started me off in journalism again. Dave Culbert, the features editor of *The Irish News*, who published it and a few others, then asked me to interview people. I did. Then I suggested I write a regular review of radio programmes. I used a pseudonym since I was signing on the dole at the time. Then I got a letter from Terry Sharkie, a BBC producer, thanking me for a review of one of his programmes and suggesting we meet. He offered me occasional work on his programme, *Sunday Sequence*.

That started a relationship with the BBC and its Religious Affairs Department that has lasted, on and off, for fifteen years, though I developed other strands of freelance journalism in that time through radio talks and newspaper articles, particularly a column in *The Belfast Telegraph*.

What I discovered, working with Terry Sharkie over the following years was that Religious Affairs journalism could be the journalism of everything, particularly the direction of change in Irish culture and politics. I often felt that the case for religious faith could have been made a lot better than the churches were making it.

Belfast was different now. The violence of the early 1970s had subsided into a routine that was much less bloody. The army was still on the streets but I was not often stopped and searched. Perhaps that was just because I was older. I think it was because the police and army now knew who everybody was and were monitoring the movements only of the paramilitary activists. By a coincidence that must be more than a coincidence, the Catholic Church was in retreat too. The religious orders of Christian Brothers and nuns were dying out. This was disguised by the enthusiasm around a visit by the Pope to Ireland which drew almost the entire population of the east westwards to see him in 1979, the year I returned. If Ireland had been floating on the Atlantic it would have been pitched into it by the sudden loss of balance.

Catholics did not accept the sexual prescriptions of celibate men any more, particularly the one that barred artificial contraception, and decided to think for themselves. The priest in Ireland was becoming something similar to what he was in India, a servant of the worshippers, rather than a leader of them. I had seen the cremation-ghat brahmin reciting his prayers at tiresome speed and the mourners toss him a few coins. I could see the priest at a funeral mass, similarly mouth theologies that few took seriously – like the promise that the dead would be restored to their bodies on the last day – then go to the pub with the mourners afterwards.

I wonder now if the decline in literal minded and obedient religion deflated the energy within the Irish republican cause. In earlier generations this tradition had been Catholic and had modelled its own assertions of the spiritual existence of an, as yet unfulfilled, republic, on the Catholic Church's assertion of One True Faith. It became harder to sustain a One True Political Faith after truth itself became negotiable. Maybe the Second Vatican Council, which accorded freedom of thought to the laity, was the first step in the Irish Peace Process.

The boys in my class at school, who had come out from under the shadow of the Brothers to find the teachings of the old chauvinist republicans familiar would, had they grown up in the new more liberal Catholicism, not have recognised it at all.

There were occasions on which Protestants too adapted their theology to the new circumstances in which they understood that the different cultures in Ireland were slowly opening up to each other. I covered a conference at which a Presbyterian minister said that he thought he could find support in the Bible for the new politics in which Northern Ireland would not have a predominantly Protestant character. His example was God telling Abraham to leave his father's house.

As a journalist, I had the luxury of asking others what they believed without ever telling them what I believed myself. This suited me because my engagement with religious ideas was a query, not a conviction. Even if I was sceptical of everything, I could see how some religious ideas were better than others.

One Christmas, I was sent to interview a retired man who had been living alone since his wife died. George was a Presbyterian with a worldly view of things. He had involved himself in trade union work when employed, and in his retirement he had put his energies into campaigning for a fairer pension.

George was a garrulous man, perhaps because he was lonely. He was shocked to discover in old age that whole days might pass without any conversation at all. He missed his wife and he had lost his faith. He said: 'I had been told that if you prayed for anything hard enough you would get it, and I pleaded with God to answer my prayer and spare my wife but he didn't.'

He quoted his Bible: 'Ask and you shall receive. Knock and it shall be opened onto you.'

'All lies. It doesn't work that way,' he said.

And I thought, 'But George, a ten year old could have told you that.'

He could not, surely, as a man who had read and conversed widely, have missed the usual theological correctives available to such simple faith as this: that God only gives you what is good for you, that he sometimes answers prayers in ways you don't recognise at first, that the door he opens isn't necessarily into a life at peace with your wife. He had pegged his hopes to an evangelical Protestantism that takes God's promise literally, that holds up wealthy evangelical preachers as evidence of God's bounty to those who serve him.

In other circumstances he might have questioned the depth of his faith, when his prayer failed, but not when he was pleading for the life of his wife. He knew he had put his heart and soul into that. Therefore the failing was in God, or there was no God.

I wasn't in the business of bringing people back to God but I thought I could have coached George in a more comfortable theology than the one that had brought him to this. Even an atheist might find that the only language for getting through to someone is one that presumes not only the existence of God but the compassion of God.

'You believe that?' he asked, when I had tried to make God more acceptable to him.

'Sometimes I do, but I certainly don't believe in a God who will give me something if I ask hard enough. God wouldn't be God if he wasn't free to ignore you. The Devil is the one who makes deals.'

And I told him about Abhay's experience. Abhay Sharaf in Deoghar, had befriended me. One day, he said; 'You know I have kissed my wife in the western way.' He explained that Indian couples don't snog.

'Did you try kissing her in the French way?'

I had to explain. His face crumpled with disgust. I didn't know at that point that Abhay's wife was dead.

'My wife and I could not have children and we visited many temples and many holy men and prayed. Then at last we performed a *yagna*, and we believed then that we would have a son. He was born thirteen months later, but in giving birth to him, my wife died. There is a price for everything,' he said.

Abhay was happy with his son, but I said to George: 'Maybe you are better off without a God who takes his cut.'

'I would have paid any price,' said George, 'for my wife to live.' Of course he would.

When I was at school the teacher would say: 'Why do you only turn to God when you need something and forget about Him the rest of the time?'

It was seen as a kind of dereliction of spiritual responsibility only to go screaming to God when you were in trouble and not to be talking to Him every day whether you were in trouble or not. The Old Testament is an account of the troubles that beset a whole race of people who turn their backs on God and ignore His law, or at least the law of the one true God. And what is that law? Do not give God a name. Do not worship idols. I take this to mean: do not accept the limits of your spiritual imagination, to worship only what you can define or depict.

Swamiji had said there were two kinds of religion and I could see his point now. The *Vedanta* tradition distinguishes between them. The one is circling in, the other is circling out. One perpetuates rebirth and brings your soul back, over and over again, to a world in which quests seek goals and questions seek answers. The other turns the soul from its love of embodied life and allows it to be free.

One is magic and the other is fatalism. One says, 'Get me out of this mess'. The other, 'Thy will not mine be done'.

And yet, are they so distinct from each other?

My mother-in-law, Betty, is a religious woman. She puts her trust in God to bring what is right for her, and she does not dispute with God when things go wrong. Yet she asks for favours.

Some years ago her husband Pat, was felled by a heart attack. It seemed likely that he would die. Betty pleaded with God: 'Spare him until the children are grown. Then if you wish to, you can take him.'

Betty told me: 'He recovered and years later he was diagnosed as having stomach cancer. I then said to God, "OK, if you want him now, he is yours."'

Then she said: 'You're laughing at this, aren't you.'

I said: 'No, I'm not. Believe me.'

Perhaps life brings everyone to the point where they plead for one last favour and then let go, and perhaps it does not always take, as the Vedantists imagine, a thousand or a billion reincarnations to reach that point. God's will, however was that Pat would recover, which he did.

There is another type of fatalism which insists that all things are predetermined and that human effort amounts to nothing. Swamiji believed that only prayer was effective in any endeavour, and that the work you did was not for the results but was a form of ritual prayer itself. In his culture the two forms of worship were distinguished yet equally regarded. He would teach me to meditate on the perfect abnegation of my own will, while at the same time teaching other people prayers and rituals to help ensure that their next child was a boy or that they would find the right wife.

He was right to acknowledge that praying out of desperation and yearning deserves respect too.

When a relationship I was in broke down, the fall was almost more calamitous than I could deal with. Helen, the woman I was in love with – mad about – had gone through an emotional breakdown and simply thrown herself at another man. I called at her home to try and sort things out and he was there. It seemed the messiest possible situation to be in.

This was a crisis because it not only denied me what I was desperate for, Helen; it also challenged me as a person to know how to let go of what I could not have. In such a moment, no matter how desperately you want what you want, part of your mind has to consider that you might be better off without it. Of course I fought my way back to her anyway. You don't always assimilate the lesson of experience just when it is put to you. It takes time for it to sink in, and by then you may of course have complicated matters further. Reading back on old diaries, I would say I have often missed the point of an experience.

When I was pining for Helen, my days seemed to last forever. I had no other preoccupation than her. I played over and over again the Springsteen song that would make me weep. I went cycling into the hills over Belfast to try to shake off the pain and I arrived at a little church which I used to pass on country walks before the Troubles. And in the pew of that church I bowed my head and begged God to get me out of this. Sort this out. I know it is not just about getting her to come back to me, I know it is about me learning something permanent about the relationships I choose. I accept that, but for now, take away the pain. Similarly, when Gerlinde ran amok through the ashram, I wasn't much into accepting the will of God then, as expressed in whatever happens: I was screaming to Him to restore my peaceful routine of spiritual indulgence.

These were moments in which my own problems with myself, my own vague sense that I was a hapless, ill-formed and irresponsible person became coherent and urgent. I do not think you walk away from moments like that unchanged, whether they occur in a church or in a bedsit flat, whether the question is directed at God, a friend, or at the night stars.

But look first for the human explanation of anything. That's what I came away from Swamiji determined to do. When I returned from India I considered living a religious life as a Catholic or other Christian. I went into churches to meditate. I went to a Quaker meeting, and I felt like a hypocrite, because I could not enter into their understanding of the man Jesus Christ. I read the gospels and I developed my own sense of what sort of person He had been, perhaps projecting something of the manipulative human power of Swamiji onto Him.

There is another character in religious literature who appeals to me in a similar way. The Mullah Nasruddin is the subject of many illuminating tales. In one, he attends a wedding feast and is turned away because he is not properly dressed. He returns with a good suit on and takes his place at the table. After the bride and groom have seated themselves and when the other guests have started to eat, Nasruddin ladles the soup over his sleeves, saying: 'Suit, this food is for you, not for me.'

The tales of Mullah Nasruddin are instructive little parables or fables, and I wonder if some of the stories in the gospels originated in the same way and got distorted by people who were too keen to take them literally. At the wedding feast of Cana, Jesus dealt with presumptuous guests who were impoverishing their host by staying for days, drinking all the wine and continuing to ask for more.

In the biblical account, Jesus simply asks for jars to be filled with water. The chief steward tastes it and approves it as the best wine yet, kept to the end. Told this way, the story is not very interesting. It is simply an account of a magic trick, as if we were told that Nasruddin's sleeves had consumed the soup with relish and remained clean, demonstrating that he was a conjuror, but leaving the brashness of his message out of account.

The story of the marriage feast of Cana is far more interesting if we believe that the water did not turn into wine. Jesus ordered the jars filled with water and fed to the obnoxious guests. The servants must have been laughing to themselves when they served it up, expecting a row, not a miracle. The guests got the message. They were no longer wanted. They were going to be fed water

142

or nothing. What were they to do about it? They could either start a quarrel at a wedding feast, or cover their humiliation and leave. The party was over.

There is a story in the *Thousand and One Nights* of a noble sheikh who affected to be deaf all his life to spare the blushes of a woman who farted in his presence; similarly, this man would effect to have tasted fine wine. Jesus was a self-sufficient man too; he did not need to share his joke with others to enjoy it, and if the others were to imagine that what they had seen was indeed water turned into wine, then he had no incentive to dissuade them of that either.

When I read of Jesus feeding the multitudes with a few loaves and fishes, I see the scary Judas moving through the crowd with his discreet knife prompting the additional contributions. The story of Martha and Mary has come down through Christian tradition as a metaphor for the tension between contemplation and action. What happened? One sat at the feet of Jesus doting on him while the other rattled dishes in the kitchen and complained that she had to do all the work alone. Jesus shut her up by saying he pre-ferred the doting. He wasn't going to get up and help with the dishes either. And this is attributed to his spiritual refinement! It could easily be read to the great discredit of Jesus, in line with his often expressed contempt for domesticity.

While living in Belfast, and not earning much money, it seemed almost an affront to my mother and father that I should insist on living apart from them, but I could not have shared a home with them. My father and I would have fought every day. My mother was depressed most of the time, though I didn't know much about depression then. She had given up trying to argue with that in-cessantly right man and virtually surrendered her will for the sake of peace.

Mum had a leg amputated when she was in her early sixties, having neglected a pain until it was gangrenous. When she was in the recovery room after surgery she said that she had seen her own mother there. Yet, towards the end, it seemed that my father might be the first to die. He had been hospitalised with swollen legs and ordered to stop drinking.

My mother ran out of serviceable lung. That is how the doctor described emphysema to me. He said, 'Imagine these floor tiles are the surface of your lung, the parts that take in oxygen, and imagine that only two or three of them work.'

In hospital she told me that a priest had come to her. 'And what he said made a lot of sense.'

She told me that she had not been to church in thirty years. I didn't know. Growing up at home I had never noticed. She worked as a night sister and would say that she went to mass in the hospital. What had finished her with faith, she told me, was the dogma of the Assumption of the Virgin Mary bodily into Heaven. She said she had simply found that ridiculous and stopped being a Catholic. The priest who had come to her asked her simply to pray that she might understand it someday and, presto, she was a Catholic again and died with the sacraments.

Her death obliged my father to start drinking again, but the illuminating part of the whole experience for me was the reminder that the community that I had lived in as a child was still there and still remembered me as a part of it.

It was a good funeral mass. Father Aidan stepped forward and said: 'I knew this woman and you all knew her too. Let's remember her.' And he talked about how much he had enjoyed visiting her and talking to her about books.

In May 1987, I went to Medjugorje in Yugoslavia with a group of pilgrims and my microphone. This was before the Balkan wars of the 1990s. I flew out with Mairead Peoples, a hotelier from near Derry who was convinced that the Virgin Mary was visiting Medjugorje every night at seven to leave a message with a group of young people there. Before the plane was in the air, Mairead was leading the rosary. Mairead would have had no trouble believing in the Assumption. She and the group with her were never happier than when they were praying. They anticipated a week of religious high spirits. Poppies bloomed in the fields of the valley floor. The hymns the pilgrims sang were all familiar from my Catholic childhood, and I was doubly nostalgic for that and for the India I was familiar with, where the breeze and the heat of January were like the atmosphere in this valley.

I shared a house with two priests and some of the other pilgrims. This was at the time that U2's album, *The Joshua Tree*, was released, and I often sat on the veranda playing the tape through my headphones while the others traipsed merrily off to mass. But what was distinctive about Medjugorje was how it recalled the sounds of my pre Vatican Council Catholic childhood. Though I could be cynical and sceptical of the story that the Virgin Mary appeared there every night to a group of teenagers, I did have a sense of calling of my own. It was a calling to sit out on the veranda at night and hear the hymns that I had not heard since I was twelve years old, and mix nostalgia with devotional rapture. I would feel that this was just the sort of moment that validated all living, the sort you would hope to recall on the day you died.

The Irish country people among the pilgrims fumbled with foreign customs. A woman at the little café opposite the church howled with laughter and annoyance when her fish and chips arrived. The fish was a whole trout which had been deep fried in olive oil, according, thought the waiter, to the precise specifications he had been given. 'I couldn't eat that,' she said. 'It's looking at me.'

In Medjugorje thousands of pilgrims gathered close to the house where they believed the Virgin Mary was appearing. They sang the old hymns like: 'Mother of Christ, Star of the Sea, pray for the wanderer, pray for me.'

'Oh, gentle, chaste and spotless maid, we sinners bring our prayer to thee; remind thy son that he has paid (as if he would have forgotten) the price of our iniquity.

'Virgin most pure, Star of the Sea, Pray for the Wanderer, pray for me.'

I was suppressing the thrill I feel in my nerves when I hear that silly song. It's that phrase, 'Pray for the wanderer', that excites me. I know what's going on when the idea is foisted upon us that virginity equates with holiness. Women are being put in their place. Yet, this music lifts and cheers me. The pilgrimage to Medjugorje was led by a giddy priest called Father McGinnity. He thought that the pilgrims wanted no greater joy than to be saying endless rosaries. I discovered this not to be strictly correct when I brought two bottles of the local ouzo back to our house one night and got the other priests drunk.

I was invited, as a journalist, into the room where the apparitions occurred. As I climbed the steps to be the last squeezed in before the door was closed, several Irish pilgrims pushed loaded carrier bags at me to bring in, stuffed with icons, cards, books. I was dripping with these. The pilgrims would bring them home and revere them as items that had been in the presence of the Virgin Mary. Two teenagers, a boy and a girl, the young visionaries, joined the fifteen-decade rosary in that room. A Franciscan priest handed the girl a folded slip of paper. She read the note and passed it to the boy. Was he giving them their instructions? It certainly seemed a strange moment to pass a message relating to anything else. The people prayed in their mingled languages.

After two hours the room hushed. The couple took up places together where we could all see them. Mary was with them. They took turns at mouthing the silent words of their prayer to her, standing side by side yet as co-ordinated as dolls, one starting to mouth the prayers when the other stopped, passing their silent prayer back and forth.

I think everyone else in the room believed that the Virgin Mary was among us, was nearly as thrilled as if they were seeing her themselves. It would have felt wrong to encrust myself with the necessary cynicism to insulate myself from the atmosphere in the room. I would have had to will it. Instead I trusted myself to recover my sanity later on.

When I started out in religious affairs broadcasting, I was surprised to find so many people making claims to visions and spiritual experiences. After a time, I realised they were so common that if I turned my energies towards recording and enumerating them, I would have no time for anything else. What was interesting was that people experienced different things depending on what their theology taught them to expect. Where many Catholics claimed to have had visions of the Virgin Mary, Protestants tended not to see things but to feel 'quickened in the spirit'.

Many of both believed strongly in spiritual healing, though among Catholics this was often through the use of a relic, and most commonly a relic of Padre Pio. In evangelical healing services, the effect would be created by the charismatic preaching or laying on of hands by a star performer. Few of either Catholics or Protestants would have treated these events as manifestations of a single category of experience, and that was because they took them literally. When the Virgin Mary appeared, it really was her, not a metaphor for anything. If an evangelical Protestant saw her descending from the clouds to talk to him, he would assume she was the devil come to lead him astray. Among the common visionaries of Irish Catholicism and Ulster evangelicalism, I met few who were burdened by any sense of mystery, however. They related to the Personal God or the person of the Virgin Mary as people with a psychology no deeper than their own.

The 'born-again-ist' proselytisers show a remarkable ignorance of the emotional range of human experience. I do not think, if I am overtaken by a rapture, as I walk through the park on a Sunday morning, as might anyone be, that it means that the Lord God of Hosts has turned his individual attention to me. I don't feel the need to define what has happened. I think it would be less likely to happen if I analysed it too much, and I know that excessive elation is madness. But rapture is natural. It is sap rising. It is happiness, and it often comes when we have something to be happy about, whether love, opportunity or money.

They tell me they have the book that tells the truth, that it is all in the Bible. I have lived in several religious cultures and all of them had their book. All I can say is that there was another salesman through here half an hour ago making the same claims and I am left with the inherited responsibility as an individual to work out for myself if there is truth in any one of them.

Few now believe that a priest can put a curse on a family, but many know that he can bring great unhappiness. The television series, *Father Ted* captured a basic truth: that many priests live stunted lives, and are preoccupied with silly things. One priest I know, who appears often in the media, has his Mensa certificate framed on his living-room wall. I scanned his CD collection for an idea of his taste. His favourite composer is Ennio Morricone. I imagine him striding across to the church in the morning humming the theme tune to *The Good the Bad and the Ugly*. Once after we had talked for hours in his home, he apologised for not having offered me tea. He said: 'I'm afraid there is no one here to make it.'

Father Hugh Quinn, who was the parish priest of Pomeroy, gave me a radio interview to explain why he did not spend his money in shops owned by Protestants. He said we should not think he was joining the sectarian boycott against Protestant businesses in protest against Orange parades but that he owed it to his congregation, who provided him with a living, to bring his custom to them. Father Hugh had a ham radio in his kitchen. He also had a pilot's licence and took flying lessons. His shelves were full of books on war, and he was thrilled by the sight of my little mini disc recorder. Everything about him suggested a life that suffered minimal distraction from play.

I have observed, incidentally, that Catholics, like Swamiji, like to find scientific validation for the things they believe, and frequently discuss them in scientific terms without disclosing the scholastic basis of their thinking. A priest sits in a seat opposite me on the train. A headline in his little newspaper announces, 'Cloned Animals Die Younger'. This news will cheer him up, for it will spare him having to explain to his congregation the theology by which we are barred from tinkering with the creation of life. It will satisfy them to know that those who befoul God's law get their comeuppance within the natural law, though there is nothing in Catholic theology to suppose that they ought.

In the same way, campaigners against contraception emphasise that condoms have tiny holes in them, that they frequently burst and that they know a doctor in the south of France or Chicago who has proven that they are no protection against Aids. This reassurance spares them the need to explain the ridiculous theology of sex.

*The Sunday Times* asked me to compile a quiz one Christmas for ministers of religion to test their familiarity with the story of the Nativity. One of the questions I asked separated the Catholics from all the others: When did Joseph and Mary begin conjugal relations? The answer, according to the gospel of Matthew, is 'some time after the child was born'. But for Roman Catholics Mary is 'ever virgin', so the Catholics all answered that Joseph and Mary didn't have sex at all. Similarly Catholics scan over the bits of text which refer to Christ's brothers. Evangelicals also did badly in the quiz, which was strange since they are committed to knowing and believing the full text of the Bible. The ones I chose just hadn't read the Holy Book as closely as they ought to have done. I quickly lost any residual sense I might have had that the clergy are superior in intelligence or even marginally more considerate of others.

The more literal-minded devotion of some evangelicals is also the more sectarian, for the more they believe the truth of what they teach, the more sure they are that others are simply wrong. The social consequences of this are calamitous. People who regard themselves as Christian mix every day in their work or at the shops with others that they assume are damned to Hell. It's hard to trust they like you despite the fact that you are the spawn of Satan.

I met dozens of clergy and formed a general rule of distinction between the Catholics and Protestants in the way they receive you into their homes. The first thing a Protestant will do after taking your coat and before escorting you into a musty living-room is discreetly point out the toilet door. That leaves you free to exercise your own judgement about whether or not to go through that door. It provides a metaphor in action for the Protestant principle of individual responsibility. The Catholic will offer you a drink, often whiskey.

I find religious services are often routine and shallow. I once covered an ecumenical 'church crawl' outside Belfast. The idea was that a mix of people of different denominations would process together round each others' churches for a brief service at each. Few if any of the clergy had a clue about how to deal with people who were not of their own Church. The Church of Ireland minister paid homage to Oliver Cromwell, a demonic figure in the Catholic imagination, and the Roman Catholic priest conducted himself with conspicuous authority over the congregation in a way that none of the other ministers had done.

Clergymen ramble; they don't think. At a wedding service once I heard a priest tell this story: 'I went out the other night hoping to see the film, *The Titanic*. But I was late, so I went into MacDonald's instead and had a hamburger. But I thought about that iceberg and the love of Tom and Mary. And you know, the greater part of an iceberg is below the surface, and that's what Tom and Mary's love is like. Most of it is below the surface.' All he could find to compare their love to was ice.

In Omagh, in August 1999, I covered a memorial service for the victims of a bomb there the year before, not for *Sunday Sequence* but for a newspaper. The other reporters wrote of a moving service. Actually I thought it was nothing of the kind. It was a trite event. The centrepiece was a gathering together of drops of water, symbolising the tears of the afflicted. God holds all our tears – that was the idea. Mothers of people who had been killed, and others, came forward to pour their symbolic tears into a bowl, and the sound system played a crude gurgle each time one of them did this. This gurgle did not even synchronise with the pouring itself. Down below, looking up, most people around me had no idea what was happening. All they saw was bad theatre.

Religion hasn't been good at expressing the hurt of people who suffered in the violence, and the media has often preferred triteness to raw feeling. Eleven died when the IRA bombed a Remembrance Day service in Enniskillen in 1987. Thirty-one, including unborn twins, died that Saturday afternoon in Omagh in 1998. I felt something like an unreserved love for the people who had suffered. Pity gripped me physically.

One of the bereaved of the Enniskillen bomb, Gordon Wilson attained moral authority by saying that he bore no hatred for the killers of his daughter. There was as much integrity sometimes in victims who made no such statements, or those who vented their rage. There is nothing as convincing as raw passion. Rage, the emotional expression of a bereaved person, seems more honest than the emotional control of a decent person trying to find the ability to forgive. The mother of a man shot dead at his work says: 'I hope his killer roasts in Hell, for my son died with a pure soul and a clean heart.'

That was not compromised with any decent effort to be Christian.

On a morning programme, Lawrence Rush, whose wife was killed in the Omagh bomb, spoke of his hurt. He said: 'I clean my own shirts. I come into the house and there is no sound of rattling in the kitchen. I don't kiss anybody.' This was the voice of humanity more coherent and convincing than the voice of God.

The BBC, after Gordon Wilson, trawled among the victims for forgiveness. It was an ugly thing to watch. Mr Wilson had created a new type of story to be sought out, the bereaved who forgive. A reporter going to the scene of a murder went equipped with the knowledge that if he brought back a sample of forgiveness, it would make the top line of the story.

'The father of the man murdered this morning has called for prayers for his son's killers.'

That made a better line than: 'The father of the man murdered this morning is witless with grief and could not speak to our reporter.'

If the bereaved said: 'I hope my son's killers roast in Hell; I hope they die like dogs. I wish they could be erased from the earth, for it would be better for all of us if they had never been born' – if he said something like that, it might be edited out. Sure he did not really know what he was saying.

After the Shankill bomb in which nine died, I vox-popped people in the Antrim Road nearby. A young mother pushing a pram said: 'What do they expect?' I said, 'Innocent people died there.' She said: 'Well they killed our innocent people, so they are only getting their own back.' We decided not to broadcast that. Why? I don't really know why. Just because it was too blunt. The woman's logic was stupid. Our listeners could have been trusted to see that. Maybe we should have let them hear it.

Many producers are motivated by a wish to protect interviewees from their own candour and this can be funny. Once I interviewed a nun at her stall selling the handicrafts of her sisters. She had little kits in leather pouches that priests could carry with them in the car. These contained the sacramental oils. I was struck by the pattern in a blue chasuble, the robe for a priest to wear during mass.

'It represents life,' she said. The pattern was of little bulbs or eyes with long tails, shimmering in all directions across the chest. 'Rays of life,' she said.

'They are sperm, aren't they?'

'Yes,' she said. My producer cut that out to spare her what he presumed was my mischief. He doubted the nun had understood what she was saying.

In Ireland, some of those who presumed to lead us to God were discovered in the 1990s to be raping children. The story broke in the courts and then in the media that Father Brendan Smyth had been shunted from place to place by his seniors in the Norbertine order, when complaints were made that he had molested small boys and girls. Instead of getting him arrested, the Church simply moved him on to protect its own. There was theological good reason, but I have never heard the Church make the case that if priests suffered from temptation to sin, then the best formula for dealing with that was their own discipline and prayer. Indeed if theirs was not the best formula, what business had they offering a route to salvation at all? Would they not have been better referring us all to social workers, psychiatrists and the police instead of inviting us to the sacraments?

More cases emerged and this raised the possibility that the Church was a refuge for paedophiles who had entered more for the access it gave them to children than for their own spiritual welfare or for anyone else's. People began to wonder if the Church had inadvertently provided a career prospect within which the paedophile might disguise his predations on children as spiritual solicitude. If that was the case, then there would be proportionately more paedophiles in the Church than in other areas of life, and every priest who worked with children would have to have the purity of his commitment tested.

Catholics were appalled, and some simply broke their ties with the Church. Others rallied to defend the institution. Father Damian Curran had been a priest on the Falls Road in Belfast. He took boys to a house in Ardglass on the southern coast of County Down, drank beer with them and took them into his bed. One night a boy resisted him and Father Curran beat him. The boy escaped and ran for help.

The novena at Clonard monastery coincided with the trial, so I went to meet worshippers coming away from a morning mass. This was within one mile of the church in which Father Curran had served. Many of those I spoke to would have been members of Father Curran's congregation. I had my tape recorder with me, to record comments for the mid-day *Talkback* programme. I asked people what their opinion was of Father Curran. Many simply refused to speak. Some were angry with him and glad that he was in jail, but as many were angry with me that I should attract criticism of him. 'The devil puts more work into tempting the holy men. We shall remember him in our prayers. Anyone can fall from grace. None of us is perfect.'

I suppose that is the Christian response, to forgive the sinner seven times seven. But what is easier to believe, that these people were heroically tolerant Christians or that they preferred simply to remain blind to facts which would challenge their faith in the Church?

There was no need for me to be surprised by the latitude given to holy men however, after my having conceded so much to Swamiji.

As a religious affairs journalist I moved freely between the Protestant and Catholic Churches, and made my own observations of both of them. Whatever questions I asked, were asked as a journalist, not as a member or a rival. The whole world knows Northern Ireland as characterised by the tension between these traditions.

For the most fundamentalist evangelicals, the great evil in this world is the Catholic Church. Some see it as a Satan inspired movement, misrepresenting the Bible, and depriving souls of salvation by deluding them. In recent years the Presbyterian Church has debated whether the Pope is the Anti-Christ or not and could not come to agreement on the question. The evangelicals believe they harbour the sole truth about God's plan for us and God's doings among us. They cannot accommodate the possibility that God might be outside the range of their imagination, that people of other faiths may be making their own equally respectable efforts to acquaint themselves with the same inaccessible and infinite being who is the foundation of the entire knowable and unknowable universes of time, matter and consciousness.

A Presbyterian minister told me a story about the ways in which religious absolutism competed with human decency. He was a chaplain at the university in Belfast, and passed his mornings in the little coffee bar there. One day a Catholic man came in and introduced himself. He said: 'I have a big favour to ask you, and you can say no, if you must and that will be OK, but I have to ask.'

The minister was curious. He asked the man to sit down, called for a coffee for him and prepared himself to listen. The Catholic man's story was this: 'My sister married a Presbyterian man. He died the day before yesterday at work. A lorry backed into him and crushed him against the wall. You can imagine how distraught she is, how distressed we all are. Now, we want a funeral for him that can include both sides of the family, the Catholic and the Presbyterian. The trouble is, we can't find a Presbyterian minister to represent the Presbyterian side of this family, our family.'

'It would be normal,' said the chaplain, 'to ask his own minister.'

'We have done,' said the Catholic man, 'and he has refused to attend alongside a Catholic priest. It's OK, we used to have the same rule ourselves, and if nothing can be done, then that's how it is. What do you think?'

What did he think? He thought it was embarrassing to have someone suppose he would refuse to pray over the grave of a dead man for the comfort of his family. He had never refused before. He could hardly blame the Catholic man himself for expecting so little when the first minister, having weighed his own proud theology in the balance against human decency, had found it a far more significant thing. His own theology, within the same Church, presented no bar to praying in the company of a Catholic priest.

For evangelicals, to judge by the way they speak of God, He is someone a bit like your grandfather, someone who can be pleased by their endeavours, prevailed upon by their prayers, but not very likely by anyone else's prayers. They absolve themselves of all responsibility, retreat into the fantasy that, by praying for us all to be saved, they are doing something worthwhile, working to make a difference, that prayer alone fulfils their responsibilities to help end the sectarian conflict in Northern Ireland. Shored up by the fantasy that they have some one-on-one relationship with God that the rest of us would not understand, they explain their aversion to Catholicism and Irishness by their theology and deny all prejudice. They absolve themselves of any sectarianism or even political ideology by asserting that their faith describes the simple truth which the rest of us have no option but to accept or be damned.

Dawson Baillie, as one of twelve grand masters of the Orange Order, himself representing Belfast, rejected the claim that he was anti-Catholic in terms that confirm that he regards Catholics as ignorant people in need of his help. He said, 'but we love Catholics and pray for their salvation.' He trusts that if they do not give up their heathen ways and adopt his religion, they will go to Hell. And I am left wondering if some see much sin in trying to burn Catholics, when God is going to burn them anyway. By their theology, the Catholics incinerated in their homes by Loyalist petrol bombs are still burning! Evangelical Protestants in Northern Ireland frequently argue that the only answer to the problem of inter-communal violence is that all should be 'born again'. Unless all come to agree, there will be no peace, and the ones who have no need to change, being right already, are themselves. In this way they waive any responsibility to understand the political causes of violence, and their own present or past contribution to them.

In my journalism I often gave offence to literal minded Christians. They let me know it in letters to me. Here's one that arrived about the time I am writing this: 'Malachi! You may feel free to write or talk in blasphemous tones regarding the Lord Jesus Christ, but remember there's a day coming when you will stand at the Great White Throne of Judgement and answer for your sins. What a day of remorse for you and many like you to find that when the Lord Jesus Christ returns (could be at any moment) that you are left behind for judgement, or if you die – Hell will be your doom.'

As far as the writer of this letter was concerned, he had done what he could to save me and the thought of my burning eternally would be no further burden on his conscience; indeed I imagine he expects his own eternity in Heaven will be all the sweeter for relishing the thought that I am burning below. I reject the men of God, the spirit police who would regulate my life according to their sense of my place in God's universe. There was one of them at Harryville on the night I covered the picket of the mass. Pastor Alan Campbell predicted Hell fire for the heathens in the 'mass house' and the ecumenically minded Christians who supported them. Mr Campbell recorded a sermon in which he defended the mob at Harryville against the charge that they were thugs. He recognised me there. He said in one of his sermons afterwards: 'If the Protestants were the violent thugs and hooligans they were made out to be, one of the *Telegraph* reporters, the Romanist Malachi O'Doherty, was parked in a car adjacent to where I was. Everybody clearly recognised him in the crowd yet no attempt was made to molest him. If they had really been this baying mob of hooligans, that's what would have happened. That was not the case.'

Proof for him that the mob was moderate was that members of it could walk past me afterwards and not succumb to the need to hit me. Another Orangeman, Clifford Smyth, wrote a book claiming that the boycott of Protestant businesses by Catholics, after disputes about Orange parades through Catholic areas, had been foretold in the Bible. He concluded that the only hope of averting civil war was that Catholics might become evangelical-minded Christians, like himself. Blaming war on the heretic is an old custom.

I had come to believe that all religions were like little boys peeing at the sky. It was ludicrous for either to claim he had got closer to the target than the other. Faith was a human aspiration, rewarded certainly by deep stirrings and rapturous imaginings, but never grasping a truth so sure that it could usurp someone else's. Little boys do not wet the sky and Churches come appreciably no closer than each other to God, yet in Northern Ireland grave insults are predicated on the claim that they do.

Among Protestants in Northern Ireland, the paragon of the raging spiritual leader is Ian Paisley, the moderator of the Free Presbyterian Church in Belfast. Dr Paisley has a world-wide reputation as a rabble-rouser: he is the personification of Protestant anger in Northern Ireland. Far from being frightened by his anger, his followers love it. They do not see his brusque rages as a taint on his claim to be able to guide them to salvation, but as an affirmation of it. His anger is righteous and it is biblical. Paisley believes his job is to contest the spread of the Roman Catholic Church. He tests the validity of other Protestant Churches by their enthusiasm for that same task and by their adherence to the King James Bible which he takes for literal history. There is nothing that makes Dr Paisley happier than the prospect of winning a soul away from Rome and setting it on the path to salvation.

I met him in his home shortly after his seventieth birthday, to interview him about his ill-founded claims that the Irish Republic had practised genocide against Protestants living there. As we talked in his living-room, he stroked the head of a near life-size ceramic cheetah and set about explaining to me that many Catholics had come to his Church and been converted. He was assuming that I was a Catholic and he was getting quickly down to offering me the hope of salvation. Whatever the point of our interview, saving me was more important. He wanted a stab at that first. We have met many times, and he has always thrown me that lifeline. He cares.

Paisley seemed extreme when he was simply doing a pastor's job, which is to convince people that they will be happier in his

Church than in any other and more assured of Heaven. No Catholic leader was doing the same thing. Catholic proselytising has stopped, and Paisley was like a boxer in the ring who still swipes to knock out, long after his opponent has withdrawn to his corner. He once heckled Pope John Paul II in the European Parliament in Brussels and bellowed at him when he tried to begin his address. For Paisley, this was just another round in an ancient struggle. It would not have occurred to him that the Pope himself might not have seen it that way, might not even have known who he was, or that the other parliamentarians witnessing this might be merely annoyed at his bad manners. Paisley has a colossal temper and a warm sense of humour too, and much like Swamiji, he leaves people around him slightly off guard. They are not to know which side of him they will see when they meet him.

I called at his office once and he opened the front door to me himself. 'Ha.'

It was little more than a grunt. He wanted to frighten me, and he is always like that on the phone too. He will be astonishingly blunt when he answers a call. 'Yes? What do you want?'

At his office door I watched three nervous men come out and gather round him to serve his needs. They seemed anxious that they had let him down by not being prompt enough to get to the door before him. This was nothing to me. The abuse that people will accept depends on their faith, and if they see people as masters over them, accorded roles by God, then they will accede to their bullying, as I acceded to Kipperhead and Swamiji. I don't care if Ian Paisley likes me or not, and that makes it easier to deal with him.

I just smiled back at his scowl and said 'Hello', and the fearsome giant broke into a warm smile. Perhaps my experience with Swamiji and Kipperhead and indeed with my own father, has taught me not to fear such bullies. They would have you believe that their gruffness is a form of humour, indeed of affection. My father's welcome when I returned from India, not having seen me in seven years, was the same kind of snarl that dares you to break through and be friends. 'I'm a better fucking man than you are, any day of the week,' he said.

I had gone to speak to Paisley about Ballymena, and the subject of dialect came up. I asked him if he had seen a television programme the night before, in which the poet Seamus Heaney had discussed the different dialects of Bellaghy and Castledawson, neighbouring towns close to where Heaney had grown up. Paisley was delighted by some of the detail I reported from the programme. I talked also about my father's use of dialect and asked him if he knew the word 'gulpin'. A gulpin is a fool, a naïve country person. Paisley nearly leapt out of his seat like a child getting a present. 'Gulpin!' he roared. 'It's a long time since I have used that word,' and he mimicked how he might use it soon. 'What sort of gulpin does the Prime Minister take me for?'

While I was with Paisley his phone rang. The caller was a woman whose husband had just died. She wanted him to come to the funeral. He was having to tell her that he could not spare the time and he was reassuring her that her husband was happy now.

'He was a very good man and you can be assured that he is well set,' he told her. I took him to mean by this that she could trust that the man was in Heaven with God. 'You need have no worry on that account. Now, shall we have a prayer?'

And he launched into a prayer with her. I switched off my machine and bowed my head while he was praying, so I have missed the precise words, but he gave her a vigorous prayer. He commended the soul to God and asked for nothing. Catholics pray for the forgiveness of the sins of the deceased, Protestants let God make up His own mind on that. I came away from there thinking that if I was weak on a hospital bed, I would rather have a pastor like Paisley with a bit of physical presence about him than some of the wimps I have met in cloth.

Catholic prayer and Protestant prayer are not the same thing, and one of the differences is that Catholics are more ready to call on God to change His mind about something, while evangelical Protestants, trusting that they are in God's hands already, tend to simply express their pleasure with that arrangement. A former Catholic Primate, Cardinal Tomás Ó Fiaich caused unintentional offence to the families of victims of an IRA bomb, by calling for prayers for the dead in Catholic churches. The families of many of these people believed they were already saved and therefore had no need of those prayers. Indeed a prayer pleading with God to admit a soul into Heaven amounted to a public statement of doubt that that soul was in Heaven already. This was offensive to families who believed that the dead person had already found salvation while alive.

I phoned Paisley during one of the political crises that dogged the Good Friday Agreement and caught him in a talkative mood. He said: 'I was talking to Lord Hailsham the other day, and I said to him: "You know there is a marvellous word in the Bible and it is the word grace." I said: "Think about that; it is free, it is undeserved and it is from God. You need that," I said. I need it too, and you need it Malachi.'

Paisley is not a charlatan. He regards it as simple good manners to offer you the chance of salvation. Kipperhead and Swamiji were of this type. They were aggressive and absolutist religious champions who insisted that they were right and dared anyone to say they were wrong. They lived in a narrowly circumscribed universe in which God is personal, straight in his dealings and near at hand. Paisley has almost no connection with the wider culture he was born into. A pastor who has worked with him told me a story to illustrate this. There was a calendar for sale in a shop in Derry which depicted Ian Paisley in his doctoral robes. The joke in Derry was that a small boy had asked the man behind the counter how much the 'Batman' calendar cost. That in itself was funny enough to be passed on. This pastor later met Ian Paisley and two co-workers in Belfast and shared the joke with them. Ian Paisley didn't get it. 'Who's Batman?' he asked.

I sat in the campaign car with him as he toured Castlereagh Borough canvassing votes against the council's ice rink being allowed to open on Sundays. Paisley's political sidekick Peter Robinson was the chairperson of the council and himself a Born Again Christian committed to the holiness of the Sabbath. His financial advisors warned him that the rink would have to open seven days a week to pay its way, and Robinson had passed the question on to the electorate in a referendum which was inevitably going to place the sanctity of the Sabbath below the right to skate on a Sunday.

Paisley toured the area all day long with the Reverend David McIlveen and a police protection squad in the car behind them, and he spoke incessantly into a microphone calling on people to come out and vote against the Sunday opening. He stopped off at several voting centres and the people there swarmed round him.

I asked a woman as the big man was leaving if she was going to vote as he wanted her to. 'Not at all,' she said. But she would not have missed the chance to meet him and shake his hand. Then, in late afternoon he handed the microphone to McIlveen. 'I wonder would you take over? I think these things radiate something which dries up the mouth after a time.'

He could not see that his dry mouth was due to any weakness in himself. He did not consider the possibility that he was simply tired of talking. Even Jesus conceded that the spirit might sometimes be willing and the flesh weak. Not Ian Paisley's flesh. If it was failing, there had to be some explanation outside himself for that.

It was like something Swamiji would have said.

Swamiji had the marks of clerical eccentricity too, the marks of a man who has spent too much of his life being deferred to and who has never had to adapt to social mores. As I sat out reading, or just quietly with my thoughts, I might know that he was in his cottage in the other corner of the ashram, by his occasional Gah-heeeeee, loud enough to scare the monkeys. He had no thought at all of how this affected others around him. It refreshed him. That was what it was for. He would perform this *rechak* on a railway station platform or a city street. Or was he announcing himself to the world?

Swamiji was a performer. Though he did not expect his oddities to affect anyone's impression of him, he regulated his charm with great care. His Sunday morning sermons at the ashram were almost hypnotic. He could speak for an hour without pause, and this alone amazed people. He punctuated his storytelling with chuckles and scowls. He might be telling people that the westerners were full of sin, unclean, and took many wives, and that women who left their husbands were fit only for a life of prostitution; he might be telling some story from the *Puranas* of the behaviour of gods, as if it were simple history. For him the battle of Kurukshetra, at which the incarnate God drove a chariot, recounted in the *Bhagavad Gita*, was as relevant as the partition of India and Pakistan. He was mad, but he was fascinating. His followers loved him and feared him. They believed that the light of God was in him. He could have taught most clergy I know in Ireland a trick or two.

Being Hindu, Swamiji should not have proselytised. His *Gita* told him that all religions were valid ways to God. I think if he had been born in Ireland, he might have found a place for himself as a charismatic evangelical. He would have had the faithful eating out of his hands in the darklands of Ulster.

Paisley and the Ulster evangelicals, like Swamiji, believed in the conversion experience. They believed that God might be invited directly into their hearts and His presence felt there. To Paisley, this was the experience of being Born Again. It finalised one's relationship with God. To Swamiji that submission might have been one of many steps between the first call to a life of devotion and the final absorption.

Evangelicals were people who had the impertinence to proselytise, who sat beside you on buses and wanted to talk about Jesus. Even at work, they wanted to talk about Jesus. I saw them gathered on city centre street corners declaring themselves saved by the blood of the Lamb and telling me that my worthless life was leading only to Hell. They were heartened by their experience. I do not doubt that they experience enthralment. Others too might enjoy such moments of elevation and conviction as reassure the evangelicals that they are the chosen of God but choose not to define them; or they baulk before any challenge to define them. The atheist may have such moments of rapture as persuade the Christian evangelicals of their intimacy with God. Of course, the evangelical will say that it cannot be the same thing or it would have the same effects, and there is no way to prove that one person's emotion is the same as another's.

I was a tourist on a gondola going through Venice in high summer when the city was horribly cluttered. I was uncomfortably seated at the brow and several times we met congestion among other boats on the canals. Yet, once or twice we moved into a quiet, narrower stretch. The air was cooler there. We glided, and the church bells began to ring at noon, and I was as happy as I have ever been, but why? I have no need to attribute any of that peace to God, any more than I would attribute the material facts of any day to God. An ordinary beautiful pleasure of the senses is not to be undervalued, nor is a moment that says 'This world is good', though I doubt that those feelings would have come to me if I had had a toothache. Swamiji or Guatama Buddha would have said this was a delusion, a false happiness found in the wrong place. Some would say moments like that are in fact evidence of God's closeness. I think there are moments of elevation and harmony in the normal range of human experience, and that they keep us going, remind us that it is better to be alive than dead.

Who is to say if the aesthetic rapture and the devotional rapture are different. I have seen choristers weeping as they sing the 'Ruht Wohl' of Bach's *St John's Passion*. Are they moved by the music or by the contemplation of Christ in his tomb? In India one night I felt entirely removed from my body. I could not be dissuaded of that experience; it did happen, but what does it mean? – that there is a God, or only that consciousness, when it aspires ahead of itself, aspires with purpose, as the libido wants orgasm before it knows what orgasm is?

One of the best accounts of religious experience by a northern Irish writer is C. S. Lewis' *Surprised by Joy*. The joy described by Lewis appears to be a nostalgia for simplicity and clarity. He is not describing something to be sought out, but something that is a by-product of his concentration on something else and which takes him by surprise. The author of *The Cloud of Unknowing* might have understood this. He asks the contemplative to hide from God. He did not believe enthralment to be the proper object of contemplation. That would come only like the easing of an ache in the bones, after climbing a mountain. You do not climb to feel that physical relief, you climb it to get to the top, but the relief rewards your efforts.

Devout people scrutinise their interior being for signs that God is moving there. For them, depression is the absence of God, the dark night of the soul, and a sense of well-being is the grace of God, nothing to do with, say, the smooth functioning of the bowels. Contemplation sensitises them to the most gentle changes in mood and refines their perceptions of natural beauty and music because they take time to dwell on these things and locate God in them. Their joy is a taunt from within to be wiser and better, to be larger than the selfish self. It is a lust to embrace the whole sky. Why do we have this if we can do nothing with it? If this is a prompting that cannot be gratified, it is the only one of its kind we know. Yet there is something gratifying even just in feeling it. It seems sometimes to be an aching nostalgia for simplicity and innocence. If simplicity and innocence are unattainable, then we are being toyed with by our own hearts and these feelings are superfluous to a natural healthy life.

If the joy of C.S. Lewis is a convincing apprehension of the absolute, which is what he took it for, an affirmation that life has purpose and direction, what are we to make of the other convincing vision, which might be called the horror?

There are times when we appear to know with unshakeable conviction that life is a perpetual disappointment, that nothing good can ever endure, that all our hopes are pointless. Lewis felt this too, and wrote of it after his wife died. This horror can be a reaction to experience, but it too can come in the sudden epiphanic form of Lewis' joy, sudden, apparently unconnected to the thoughts and interactions of the moment. An ordinary day may suddenly be darkened by a conviction that arrives unsought, a sagging of the spirits and a clarity of understanding in which the only tenable truth is mortality and loss, in which all ambition becomes dust.

This horror has the same ecstatic quality as the joy, the same detachment from the day and the same participation in some credibly more objective overview of life and nature. The message of the horror is also reasonably more defensible than the joyful one, because it seems affirmed by the reality of evil. It says that life is suffering. Do not children die of cancer? Do not wars intervene and makes our dreams meaningless? Do not some people who invest all their hopes in stability, routine and hard work, slowly accumulating some security for themselves by their patience and endeavour, find themselves destroyed by a bomb or a bug? Buddha made this realisation of total suffering the starting point of his theory. Far from joy being the beginning of faith, as it was for Lewis, for the renunciant Buddhist or Hindu it is horror. Their insight is that all desire leads downward into grief, and that grief and loss further delude us. Only when we are sickened with this life do we inquire into the nature of life and existence. The Buddhist recoils from ordinary domestic life like an alcoholic reaching rock bottom and swearing off drink. Nowadays we tell people who dwell on these things that they take life too seriously.

Then I found myself burying my sister Brid and thinking about these things again. She died young because she was a heavy drinker. She had had pneumonia and had not been treated for it. When she became so sick that she lost her appetite for drinking she slid into *delirium tremens*. When her friend took her to hospital, Brid believed she was talking to our dead mother. Mum, when she was in a similar crisis, having a leg amputated, saw and talked to her own mother. I was so angry about alcoholism that I resolved for a moment to have an honest funeral, to speak plainly about what had happened, and then I simply lost that determination and felt that the right thing was to go along with what people in my half-hearted Catholic world expected.

The priest led prayers for my sister who, he said, had 'lived by the word of God'. Lying in her coffin, dressed in a ridiculous blue gown with a picture of the Virgin Mary on the front, wearing lip-stick for the first time in thirty years, she would have cackled with laughter.

I felt I was seeing things through Brid's sense of humour. At the hospital a tactless young clergyman came to me and rested his hand on my shoulder. I suddenly recalled a similar incident at my mother's wake. Brid had been sitting on the sofa. An old priest came to stand in front of her and rested his hands on her head, as if he thought he was spiritually healing her hurt.

Brid turned to me with an expression of exaggerated bewilder-ment or self-deprecating embarrassment. We both fought not to laugh. The funniest thing for me was the fight between a blush and a guffaw that was clear on her face. That image lightened for me the day that Brid died fourteen years later. Her genius was for demolishing reverence with a glance or a joke, a genius with which she abused me in my reverential youth. I have seen her with a child in her lap singing, 'Red and yellow, black or white, Jesus doesn't give a shite, Jesus loves the little children of the world.'

People of faith said to me: 'At least now Brid is at peace.'

These words annoyed me and were no comfort to me. Did they mean simply: 'At least now she is dead, and her troubled life is over?' I could see that for myself. Or did they mean: 'She is in Heaven now and happy?' Well, I didn't believe that either. My im-mersion in Hinduism prompts me to a psychological model that outspans a single life. It prompts me to think of Brid as a soul who will reincarnate, who must resolve experiences before she can be free. She did not learn in this life; therefore she must keep reincarnating until she does learn. Why would I find that a more comforting thought than that she might now simply be absolved of all her trouble and given peace, as if she could step out of life, into the arms of God, with a 'Whew, you really shook me up there', and rest contented forever? I suppose it is because I cannot imagine a contentedness that is not earned by experience nor do I want to. And why don't I want to?

The Christian idea is that the grace of God puts everything right, and that it comes whether it is earned or not. The Ulster evangelical believes you pay for everything in this world, but one thing alone is free, God's grace. This runs right through the gospels. Am I so hard-hearted and mechanistic that I cannot believe in a divine love that waives its own laws?

A year later my father died. That's the thing about death, it keeps on happening whatever else does or doesn't. He had been going into hospital practically every year to dry out and learn to walk again. He passed through long delusional phases when he thought that animals were swarming the ward. There was always a distinctive feel to these delusions. He was not himself. Then occasionally he was himself, but confused. One night I visited him with my brother Brian. Dad complained that Gerry Adams, the Sinn Féin leader, had been working on the ward all day in a white coat.

'What do they have him in here for? Sure he's not a doctor.'

Brian said; 'I'm sure it wasn't really Gerry Adams you saw.'

And Barney snapped at him. 'For fuck's sake, do you think I don't know Gerry Adams when I see him!'

On coming out after one of these treatments he had a fall. I was walking with him, and I should have been able to prevent that and felt small for my ineptitude.

Every time he was in hospital, he lost his swallow and every time nearly drowned on his food. In the end, as with Mum, there simply wasn't enough air in the world for him and he died exhausted trying to get more of it. I doubt if his death would have been more ungainly had he been tortured for a week then dispatched with a bullet.

His sons carried his coffin up the street they had played in as children, followed by the grown up children they had played and fought with, along the route their first holy communion parade had followed – though in a much more crowded world – watched by neighbours who had come in more recent decades to the estate and perhaps wondered who we all were.

The church was full for his mass.

The girls in the off-licence had his picture framed and hung in their tea-room.

That was the year of deaths; my father's brother, an aunt. Death brings us back into church. Death is what religion is about. Death also frees each successive generation to think and learn. It lifts the weight of parental authority off our shoulders. It is nature's rebuttal of tradition.

Then one day I got an e-mail from an academic researching Austrian women dramatists. He told me that Gerlinde Obermeir had committed suicide in 1984, within a year of the last time I had seen her, and I almost felt spared. Had her death landed in my lap at the time, it might have been such a shock as to change the direction of my life since then.

Hermann Hesse wrote a story called 'Siddharta' about a young *saddhu* who is distracted by real life, gets married and has children and then wakes up to his vocation, realising that everything in between was an illusion. This was the opposite. I woke up to my past with the news about Gerlinde having died so long ago, but the gap did not close between that time and then. I had moved on.

Then I learned that she had shot herself in the bath and I felt sick in my stomach for days.

Death is what religion is all about.

Those who think about death think about destiny and ask what the point of life is, as Buddha did. We live in a horribly vulnerable condition. In 1970, my biggest fear was that I might be shot or blown up. Thirty years later, I live in dread of cancer, road traffic and the passage of time. Something will get me, and it seems a random matter. My father might as easily have survived his last spell in hospital as he survived the others. What would have made the difference? Maybe he would have lived into his nineties had he not gone into hospital at all. He went in angry and spirited and demanding treatment and he was immobile within two days.

Did Gerlinde plan to die that night or did the cruel notion overtake her? Would she have been able to resist it if there had not been a gun at hand? Even a suicide can have an element of accident in it.

It is the fickleness of death that suggests there is no meaning to life at all, that nothing in me as a person is valued by the cosmos. Nothing out there cares whether I die at nine or at ninety-nine.

Yet, the inevitability of death by some chance event, whether a blood clot or a bullet, has a grounded certainty that nothing else in life has. If there is a starting point to any reasoning about what is to be made of life, it has to be the acceptance that it ends and that it may end in a horribly unexpected way.

Reflections on death can produce the same self-effacement that religion teaches, even without considering an after-life and a God. Death bleeds into life and makes all things transient. Unless I soberly contemplate my mortality I am deluded. What point then in seeking to be rich? Better to spend life simply in the contemplation of its transience, with no thought for the future. Death's challenge is a challenge to hope and pride. What point is there in giving your life to effort when results don't last and you don't either? It is also a challenge to die well, rather than to die late, for death can be messy and random. It is a perpetual fact of life, not something whose consideration can be deferred, except at the risk of being taken by surprise, unready. The adult knows not to be as excited as a child since all pleasures pass. Perhaps that is all that many religious people have been trying to explain to the immortal young. If I may die tomorrow, what value has any happiness that overlooks that? Once you focus on the fact that you will die, it hardly matters whether you suppose that something will come after. The fact is you will lose what you have.

Those who imagine a life after death in a world like this, in which they will be reunited with friends, aren't facing up to the magnitude of death. People used to give more energy than they do now to anticipating an after-life, in which they would mix again with those they knew. They don't any more. They seem now not to want more life and more consciousness after their time is up. Maybe the fantasy of a Heaven that's like a better earth is something needed by people who do not get enough life. Songs about angels seem always to be for children. Heaven appears to be the fantasy of those who see life cut short, a reassurance that the deficiency is restored. Those who grow old and bored don't need it or want it. Maybe our living longer is one of the causes of the depletion of religious interest; it is not more life in Heaven that many old people yearn for but an eternal sleep.

Some, like my father, face death in old age, with horror, wholly unprepared. When we talked with a nurse at his bedside and he seemed unconscious, he awoke with a start at the mention of death. I asked the nurse what the danger of his dying was and one eye opened wide and rebuked me with a stare. Others accept it and get impatient for it. My aunt at ninety said: 'Something has changed in this world, for I am not supposed to be here.'

Life pulls against death but death wins out not just by killing us, but by winning our assent in advance of killing us. In time the soul is sated and then bored with life. People of ninety do not yearn to go on living and learning. We bore them because they understand us and the world around them as well as they are ever going to. My mother in her last years read books not to be fascinated and informed but simply to fill the passing hours.

My father wanted nothing more from life than it had given him. It was not hunger for new experiences that made him cling on. He did not die, I think, wishing he had gone to Spain or learned to play the violin. He was just afraid of the cliff edge, I suppose, the not knowing, perhaps even of retribution against his immortal soul. He believed in God but I think he was disappointed in God and stopped going to church decades before he died. I don't fully understand that. The arrival of the Troubles deflated both my parents.

What we witness in this limited life is that it is primarily a school. We learn here. We grow older and become wiser. Some of us don't learn very well, but we all have an idea that we should. And somehow it can not be incompatible with our learning that we die.

The trouble with God is that He stays out of our affairs. If any clear policy on human destiny can be attributed to Him and His silence, it is that He has left us to get on with it ourselves. We are free to make a complete mess of this world. Every imaginable calamity has already happened and God has not intervened, a fact that has puzzled some and heartened others.

Many, perhaps most, have a sense that God is close to them and inspires them, sometimes in the most literal ways. For me, it is the literalness of these communications that makes them suspect. If an angel wrote a message on the wall in front of me, I would be appaled. When I left the room in Medjugorje where the young visionaries had spoken to the Virgin Mary, a few feet from me, I was elated. We had effectively been meditating in there for hours. I looked up at the evening sky. The light was silvery and a beam of sunlight shafted rigid towards the earth. Suddenly I saw there a photographically clear image. Viçka, one of the visionary girls, was pictured in the sky in a half-profile, the beam of light coming straight from her to the earth, like grace from Heaven, in the style of the little gaudy holy pictures we had carried in our prayer books as children. I have often seen images take this clarity for me, in woodgrain, or in a damp patch on a plaster wall, but rarely immediately. I decided that my imagination was sharing a joke with me. I worried too that it might be a psychic or spiritual vision. I did not want one that was so tacky and explicit. I did not want to believe in a God I could not credit with a little more taste.

Everywhere the human imagination grapples with the hope and idea of God and everywhere the imagination rewards its own efforts and concerns. Does that mean there is nothing else to this question of who or what is God?

Our language about God is like the language which in our dreams describes the world. In both we are insulated by metaphor from what we cannot know or must not know. Perhaps God is our fantasy friend on whom we exercise our humility and concerns. Yet if the idea of God enlarges the minds of some, it clearly contracts the minds of others. Many religious people give their lives to a God who appears to require of them that they live narrowly, without music or love or play, and shut out other people on account of their differing beliefs or social customs. They imagine a God who appears to be more concerned that they should live sexually restricted lives, or that they should attend a specific place of worship, or that they should be free to march along one particular stretch of road, than that they should grow in their capacity to love and understand.

Some serve a God who wants them to kill. Perversely the Ulster Loyalist killer Billy Wright regarded himself as serving God as Judas did, sacrificing himself into sin for the glory of God. Johnny Adair saw some role for God in his own psychopathic rationale. His slogan, displayed on a banner in his prison cell, was: 'Kill them all, let God sort them out'.

The God of some is as petty as themselves; he is the stern father with merely domestic preoccupations, one of these being that those who serve him should never be more than children. Catholicism provided consolation for this fear and that was the Virgin Mary, the mother, the one who was always on the right side of God and could sweeten his paternal temper. Like Hinduism, Catholicism provided a whole range of beings that a devotee might focus on, in the saints and angels, or in facets of God, from baby Jesus to mystic paraclete. Religion is useful to more people if it provides a range of ideas of God; and the more tight the prescription, the more limiting it is.

But is there a God, or is all our engagement with that idea merely a means of filling the deficiencies of family, replenishing parental love and rationalising earthquakes? The reductionist idea is that in our first confrontation with mystery we explained what we could not understand by personifying it. In personifying it, we enabled ourselves to talk to it. The volcano was therefore a fickle and angry god. The sun was a more dependable god, who followed routines. There are still mysterious forces in our lives, however, that invite the same tortured questioning of motive. 'Why did my child have to die?' It is a foolish question on the rational level, but no bereaved parent has ever been able to dispel it simply with logic.

And if God is myth, he is the patch we cover our broken selves with. If I need to be loved by a father to feel whole, then God can provide that for me where life did not. Sometimes in life we find coherence in our personalities, we touch something foundational, and it may be that only the idea of God can get us there because only the idea of God can complete us – unless of course we have grown up with all the love we would ever need. I didn't.

All we know of religious devotion is our own side of it, the yearning heart which brings its own great indefinable want before the great indefinable unknowable other. What affirms it is the experience that it is enthralling and liberating. The question of whether God exists remains unanswerable. The spiritual obligations are the same as the psychological obligations; they are that you should know yourself, be honest with yourself and that you should bring that honesty and knowledge to someone outside yourself. And because there is never anyone in this world in whom you can have no interest at all, then the only one to bring all to is God.

I take God to be the mirror in space of the whole self, to which nothing need ever be said, which, acknowledged, can be taken wholly for granted. God's role in my life is to accept me completely. Perhaps this is a device of my imagination, but it is an essential of my psychological make-up, maybe even a necessity imparted to me by nature. Perhaps there is an infinite all-comprehending silence. All that we can imagine of it is that it comprehends our own being and completes it, that our whole coherent selves can turn to it as to no other, with a sense of full acceptance. We should let the thing decide for itself what it is and allow ourselves to be carried by it, and give up trying to map a destination we cannot see.

So what do I believe? At least this much I think, that consciousness did not emerge out of matter as an added trick to the Darwinian repertoire, but pre-exists it perhaps, as radio signals pre-exist the radio. And just as the best radio set may not yet have been invented, we may not be the best possible or even best existing medium for the expression of consciousness or spirit. There may already be creatures in nature, that is somewhere in the universe, who express it better; we may even be on our way to expressing it better ourselves.

Which leaves me where? It leaves me still dreaming occasionally that I am walking a dirt road to the Ganges and that I have yet to arrive there. It leaves me in the porch of the church at Harryville, inclined to love but not to affirm, my faith made evident not by reasoning but by its own insistence. I side with devotional people, even if I can never manage to agree with them on the details.

I am not a Catholic. That is by choice. I was raised as one and I consciously rejected the membership of this Church that was bestowed on me before I was old enough to think. I was what church people call a lapsed Catholic, as if my not being one had come about by accident, but this had been no accident. Like many a Catholic before me, I had engaged in a struggle for understanding. It had not been easy to turn my back on my religious conditioning.

Terry Eagleton has said, in a book review in *The Irish Times*, that it might be harder for us to give up our faith if the Church had presented us with more of an intellectual challenge. He wrote: 'One of the more insidious crimes of the Irish Catholic Church has been to deprive the nation of the kind of intellectually challenging, politically relevant version of the Christian gospel which it would cost you something to reject.'

He says an autocratic Church has 'allowed its rebels to buy their atheism on the cheap ... A feat which might be less easy in the jungles of Guatemala.'

It felt to me in the church porch in Harryville that I was paying dearly for my right not to be a Catholic, now that I was beyond going into that church and joining that hymn, when I was there only as a journalist, effecting some neutrality between their piety and the mob. It's true that the intellectual argument of Irish Catholicism, as I knew it, was fairly easy to demolish. It was sport for my generation to taunt teachers with its anomalies and conundrums, though later generations saw little point in even bothering with that. But the Church has another hold on us, not on our intellect but on our feelings and on our identity.

When I was in Medjugorje with a group of women ascending a stony mountain path to a giant cross where they would pray, one of them scolded me for recording the sounds of the pilgrimage: 'Why can't you just put that thing down and be part of this?' My microphone and my notebooks have been my shield against full involvement; they have been my excuses for being there, among the praying people, not praying with them.

In India with Swamiji, I experimented with allowing a strong man to control me and direct me to God in his shadow. In return, Swamiji became all types of people to me. In the end he was not the master but the child and needed support from me that I could not give him. When I bring him back to mind now, I sometimes see that stern buccaneer, it's true, but I also see that vulnerable and curious person, shifting from one foot to the other, like a little boy working out some thought he is not ready to articulate. I see him in the windy days of January walking alongside me out that road away from Brig Ghat dressed in his silly orange headscarf over his permed hair, seeming not to know or to mind how womanly he looked. He looked like a woman too when he gathered his skirts around his haunches and squatted to pee at the side of the road. He walked in those impractical shoes, the *kharaons* with the single knob for the toes to grip, his right foot having only half a big toe, yet I have seen him leap off a wall in them, and land softly, like one well used to awkward heels.

Yet he represented the displacement of women. Women loved and served him, but he never believed that they were equal to men and he taught that it was the responsibility of the man not only to protect his wife but to discipline her. I asked him about this once and he said: 'If a husband does not chastise her, then who is to do it?'

What Swamiji gave me was not a simple masculine formula for life that I could reason with and reject, but a complex personality that I could not refuse to love. It was as paradoxical as his religious teachings: that God was *Brahman*, one without condition; and that God was Saraswati, who sat on a swan and played the *bina* as she fingered her rosary and read her book; that God was sky-clad Shiva who would wake from his sleep and destroy everything that God, Vishnu had created. Swamiji's religion allowed the free run of the imagination around all possible conceptions of God. These included the destructive woman Durga on her tiger, the garland of blood-dripping skulls around her neck; little baby Gopal, who would grow into Krishna, who spied on naked cow-girls bathing and drove the chariot of Arjuna and taught him in the heat of battle that all around him was illusion.

Emer said to Cuhoolin: 'Heed her not Cuhoolin husband mine, delusive is the bliss she offers thee.'

She called her warrior back from absorption in the unconditioned divine feminine to life with a woman of the earth, beside whom the warrior would learn all that he had yet to learn before he was fit for the life of the spirit. This is the message Jesus gave when he told his people to leave the temple and sort out their quarrels with their brother. It is actually what Swamiji told most of his followers too: go and get married, live your earth-bound lives and leave the spiritual contemplation to me. He reasoned that that was the destiny of most people and that they should get on with it, though he belittled it and imagined it to be a lesser destiny than his own.

If Swamiji's religion is true, then he may already be reincarnated and grown to adulthood in a new life. If so, I hope he has someone to hold him through the night. I hope he has discovered the comfort of touch.

An old joke in Ireland has Ian Paisley die and go to Heaven, where he is given a quiet corner with a few like-minded people to enjoy the sense of having the whole place to themselves. There is an intuition behind that joke that people get the Heaven they dream of, which is what Swamiji believed. In his cosmology, desire in the heart at the time of death determined not only the Heaven a soul would find, but the life that soul would return to earth to live, all desire had been assuaged. Did he die wanting nothing? I doubt it.

In my mother's Heaven she does not have to listen to the constant arguments of her husband and her children. She had frustrations which would draw her back to embodied life. That was clear.

Gerlinde died rejecting embodied life completely. Her last desire, framed in her heart, was, for oblivion. How does Swamiji's theory of karma cater for that? With eternal extinction? Or was that desire really for an alternative tenable life, imagined perhaps as one that started better, without a Nazi father. Her karma would bring her back here to live the life she desperately longed for instead of the one she discarded. Her Heaven may be very like my sister Brid's and my father's. I wonder if they too grab the trouble they loved or find a peace there that placates the rush to self-destruction.

Gerlinde wrote a story once about a perfectly peaceful place that you were allowed to stay in until you had worked out what you wanted most. Her character realises that all he wants is to stay there forever. At that point, according to the rules, he has to leave. That story suggests a mind that has no expectation of dependable happiness.

Will my father find whiskey, which is what he wanted most in life or the ability to be at peace without whiskey? I don't know if he ever owned up to a desire for that. Brid did. She acknowledged that she was an alcoholic and wrote it down on an application form for disability benefit. I found it in her flat.

Kipperhead, of course, will be in Heaven, probably playing handball. I see him dancing before the wall through eternity, tilting low, his hand poised almost flat backward at his ear, waiting and twitching as his eye marks the curve and sweep of the ball to

the point before him on the ground, backing off anxiously to accommodate its rise in front of him and meet it with sufficient
power to thrash it back. Handball is good exercise for caning, but
he need never cane again. He plays alone.